Activity pages that teach about the OLD TESTAMENT!

Susan L. Lingo

www.susanlingobooks.com

Show me your ways, O Lord,
teach me your paths.
—Psalm 25:4

**Choose 'n Use Activity Pages That Teach About the Old Testament**



Published by Susan Lingo Books, Loveland, Colorado 80538.


Interior design and cover by Susan L. Lingo



17 16 15 14 13 12 11 10 09 08 5 4 3 2 1
ISBN 978-1-935147-10-7
Printed in the United States of America

# Contents

## LOYAL JOSHUA ......... 69



## WISE KING DAVID ......... 87



## PRAYERFUL DANIEL ......... 107

# Introduction

## Every lesson meeds support to make learning truly memorable!

Whether you're telling a Bible story, exploring biblical characters and their qualities, or honing in on Bible skills and Scripture memory, there's nothing as good as quality, fun-to-complete activity pages to drive home the point! Most professional educators agree that learning needs a 3-step approach to occur, including:

- **Reteaching**—This step helps kids lock in learning they may have missed during your teaching time.
- **Reinforcement**—This step gives kids a chance to use what's been learned and to strengthen skills
- **Enrichment**—Enrichment allows kids to "go a step further"—it is this step that provides for fun, memorable learning.

*Choose 'n Use Activity Pages That Teach About the Old Testament* provides loads of reteaching, reinforcement, and enrichment through Bible skills, Scripture memory fun, lively games, creative crafts, recipes and snacks, and much more. From exciting background information and Bible facts, to mini character studies of all the Old Testament favorites, your kids will be delighted at the learning fun included in each chapter.

## Simply choose which pages are right for your kids—then let the learning begin!

There's something for every Old Testament lesson included in *Choose 'n Use Activity Pages That Teach About the Old Testament.* Just look at some of the key characters, themes, and biblical events included:

| CHARACTER | EVENT | THEME |
|---|---|---|
| • Noah<br>• Abraham<br>• Moses<br>• Joshua<br>• David<br>• Daniel | • the Ark<br>• Abraham's journeys<br>• Isaac's birth<br>• plagues and Red Sea<br>• The Ten Commandments<br>• manna<br>• walls of Jericho<br>• Rahab helps the spies<br>• David and Goliath<br>• David writes the psalms<br>• David the shepherd<br>• the lion's den | • obedience<br>• God's covenants<br>• faith and trust<br>• obeying God's call<br>• families<br>• a listening heart<br>• God's provision<br>• courage through God<br>• God's armor<br>• true friendship<br>• God sees inside our hearts<br>• angels<br>• worship and prayer |

## Collect the character posters for great instant reviews!

At the end of each chapter you'll discover a mini poster of a biblical character, a Scripture verse to learn, and the quality this person demonstrated through God's help. Let kids color these posters and solve the missing words in the Scripture verse by looking up the verses in their Bibles. Encourage kids to hang the posters in their rooms at home for instant reviews and reinforcement of Scripture.

Have fun choosing and using these exciting learning and activity pages with your studies of the Old Testament, its characters, themes, and Scripture verses. And remember, these pages-no matter what order you choose them—are great as:

- **Quick discussion starters!**
- **Instant take-home pages!**
- **Partner activities!**
- **Extra moment fillers!**
- **Whole class reviews!**

# OBEDIENT NOAH

**"Noah did everything just as God commanded him."** (Genesis 6:22)

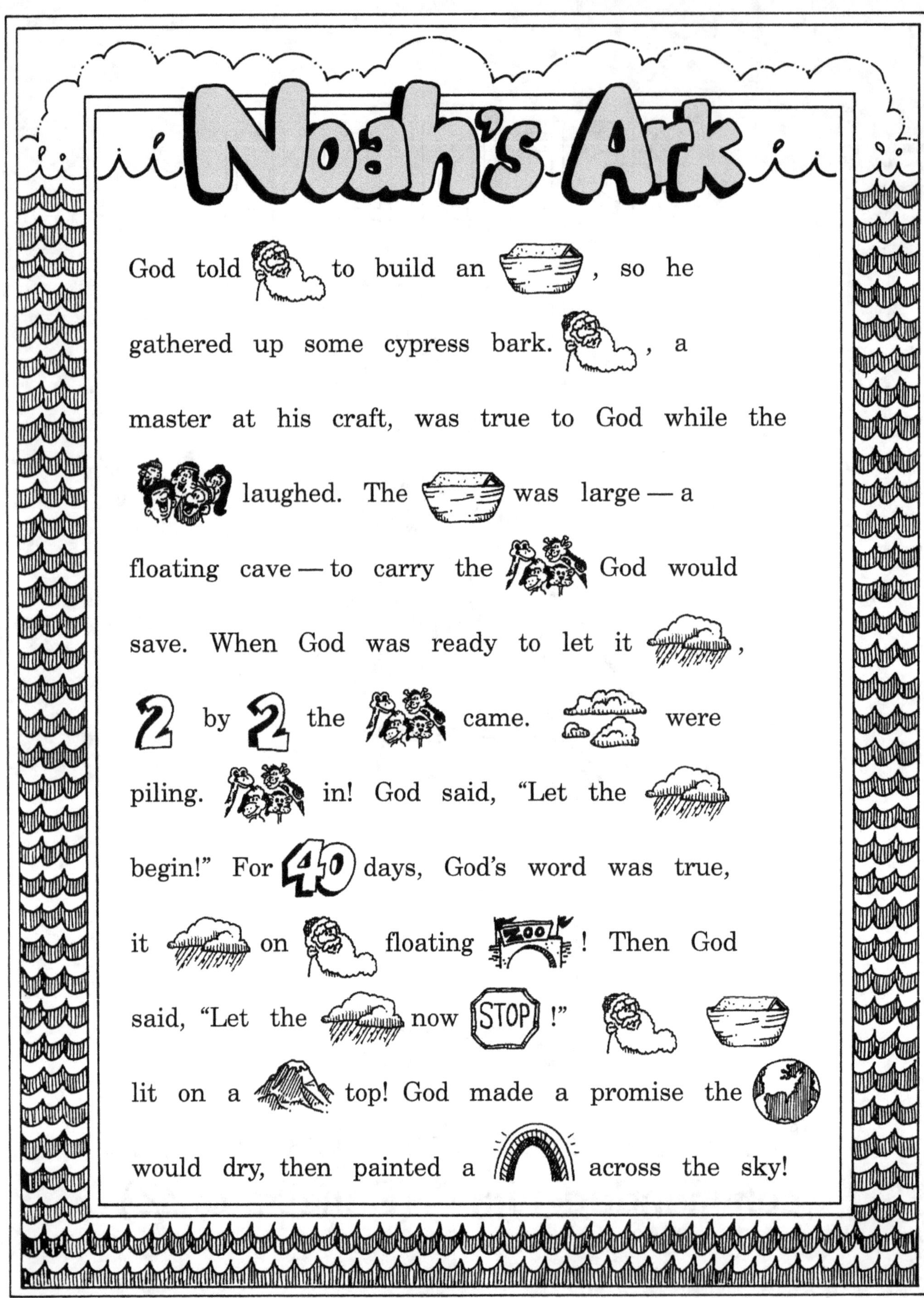
Noah's Ark
God told to build an , so he
gathered up some cypress bark. , a
master at his craft, was true to God while the
laughed. The was large — a
floating cave — to carry the God would
save. When God was ready to let it ,
2 by 2 the came. were
piling. in! God said, "Let the
begin!" For 40 days, God's word was true,
it on floating ZOO ! Then God
said, "Let the now STOP !"
lit on a top! God made a promise the
would dry, then painted a across the sky!

Because Noah loved the Lord with all his heart, he obeyed God. Memorize the following verse, and then complete the puzzle below to find out what God commanded Noah to do.

**"Noah did everything just as God commanded him."**
**Genesis 6:22 (NIV)**

To discover what it was that God commanded Noah to do, find which letter of the alphabet is missing from each of the lines below and write it in the appropriate space at the bottom of the page.

A C D E F G H I J K L M N O P Q R S T U V W X Y Z
A B C D E F G H I J K L M N O P Q R S T V W X Y Z
A B C D E F G H J K L M N O P Q R S T U V W X Y Z
A B C D E F G H I J K M N O P Q R S T U V W X Y Z
A B C E F G H I J K L M N O P Q R S T U V W X Y Z

A B C D E F G H I J K L M N O P Q R S U V W X Y Z
A B C D E F G I J K L M N O P Q R S T U V W X Y Z
A B C D F G H I J K L M N O P Q R S T U V W X Y Z

B C D E F G H I J K L M N O P Q R S T U V W X Y Z
A B C D E F G H I J K L M N O P Q S T U V W X Y Z
A B C D E F G H I J L M N O P Q R S T U V W X Y Z

_ _ _ _ _   _ _ _   _ _ _

## To assemble:

1. Photocopy, color, and cut out the animal markers below. Glue the game board to the inside of a fold.
2. Fold markers on the dotted lines and each to a penny so it will stand upright.

Directions

Use a die to roll and move your animal marker.

The first animal to the Ark is the winner!

**Teachers:** Color (or have students color) the gameboard.Then mount the game on a file folder, and laminate it to use over and over !

RACE

Start

Euphrates

River

Cool drink from the river! Move ahead 3 spaces!

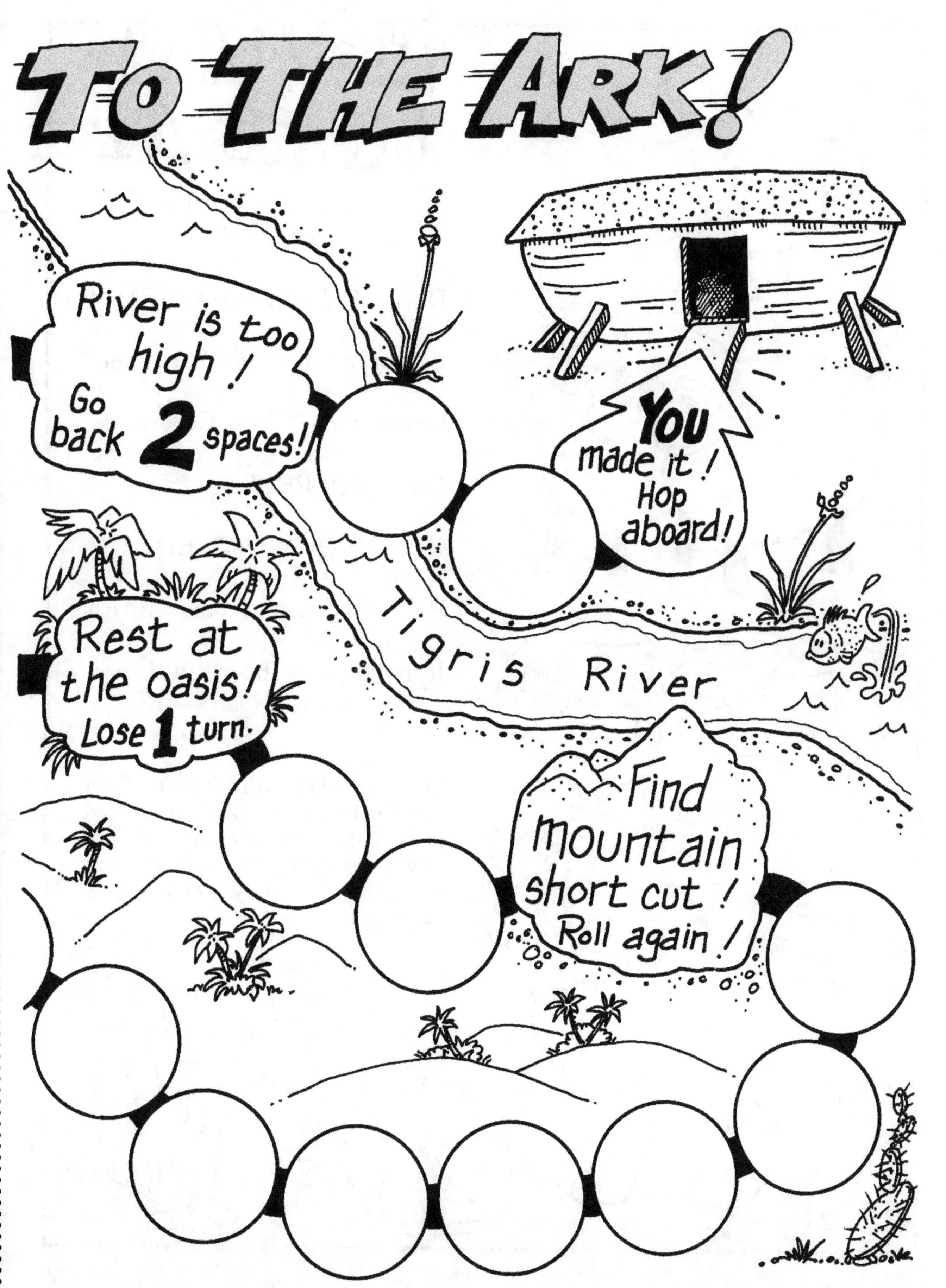
To The Ark!
River is too high! Go back 2 spaces!
You made it! Hop aboard!
Rest at the oasis! Lose 1 turn.
Tigris River
Find mountain short cut! Roll again!

# The Animals on Noah's Ark

The animals on Noah's Ark
Entered 2 by 2;

Ducks QUACK QUACKED!

Lambs cried, "Baaaaaaaaaaa!"

Doves sang, "Cooo Cooo Cooo!"

Lions ROARED!

Cats MEOWWWWWED,

Both the dogs woofed "BARK!"

It must have been quite noisy
Sailing on Noah's Ark!

The animals go with the poem. Color them, cut them out along the dotted lines, and glue them on craft sticks. Now have a puppet show while you read the poem! Can you make sounds like they do?

What animals sailed on the ark? "Two of every kind of bird, of every kind of animal and of every kind of creature that moves along the ground . . . " (Genesis 6:20, NIV).

Some of the animals are hidden below—see if you can find them!

| | | | | | | | | | |
|---|---|---|---|---|---|---|---|---|---|
| R | H | A | M | S | T | E | R | A | F |
| A | I | N | P | S | U | M | R | O | W |
| E | P | U | E | P | I | S | X | O | A |
| B | P | V | L | I | O | N | I | T | M |
| T | O | A | B | D | L | A | A | L | O |
| D | I | E | T | E | E | K | N | E | N |
| E | X | G | S | R | M | E | T | M | K |
| M | I | C | E | N | A | G | R | U | E |
| T | S | T | O | R | C | O | N | R | Y |
| E | L | E | P | H | A | N | T | M | S |

| | | | |
|---|---|---|---|
| Ant | Elephant | Lemur | Pup |
| Bear | Fox | Lion | Snake |
| Camel | Hamster | Mice | Spider |
| Deer | Hippo | Monkey | Tiger |
| Dove | Ibex | Ox | Worm |

## Food For Thought

What if you would spend a month in an ark with your favorite animals? Which animals would you pick? What food would you need to take along? How would you make them comfortable for the trip? What problems might you have to solve?

# Millie and the Thunder

Millie was a mouse. She was small and brown and had a long tail. Millie liked a lot of things. She liked hot dogs. She liked to look at stars. She liked to run and jump by the pond. She liked her tiny gray mouse doll very much, but . . . she did *not* like thunder. Millie the mouse was afraid of thunder!

One day, Millie went for a long walk. The day was full of sunshine and Millie had such a good time! She looked at pretty speckled rocks. She smelled tiny pink and blue flowers. She chased white dandelion fluffs up and down green hills! She smiled at the beautiful world and how God had planned it all, just for her!

Before she knew it, Millie was far away from her home. The day was very hot, and Millie was growing quite thirsty. "Oh! I would very much like a long cool drink of water!" she said. Millie was too far from home to get a drink there. No puddles, no drops of dew on the grass—no water anywhere to be found! "I AM thirsty!" cried Millie.

Just then, *Rrrrrrumble! Booommm!* Millie looked up into dark clouds. Where was the blue sky? Where was the sun? Had they run away so quickly, just when they were all having such fun?

*BOOM! BOOM! B OOM!*

"Thunder!" cried Millie. Her wee nose wiggled, her tiny heart pounded, her little feet ran! So afraid! So afraid! So afraid! Millie ran helter skelter, here and there, up and down looking for a place to hide. She nearly tumbled over Toad, who was sitting on a very dry lily pad. "Thunder!" cried Millie.

"Thunder!" croaked Toad. "Thunder," smiled Toad, "is part of God's plan! It brings the rain to water the land! Now my pond will be full!" Toad was happy for thunder.

*BOOM! Crrrash!* Millie raced on and almost dashed into Duck, who was waddling along in the dust. "Thunder!" cried Millie.

"Thunder!" quacked Duck. "Thunder," smiled Duck, "is part of God's plan! It brings the rain to water the land! Now I can swim in the stream!" Duck was happy for thunder.

*BOOMMM!!*

Millie trotted slower this time and plopped into Pig, who was standing in dirt. "Thunder!" said Millie.

"Thunder!" said Pig. "Thunder," smiled Pig, "is part of God's plan! It brings the rain to water the land! Now I can roll in the mud!" Pig was happy for thunder!

Millie stopped. She thought about Toad. She thought about Duck. She thought about Pig, and she thought very hard about God's plan. Suddenly Millie shouted, "I know! Thunder brings rain, and rain is water! Water to fill ponds! Water to send streams! Water to make mud! Water to DRINK! And I AM so thirsty!"

*Rrrrrumble! BOOM! CRASH!* This time Millie did not run. She happily skipped!

"Thunder," smiled Millie, "is part of God's plan! It brings the rain to water the land! Now I can finally have a drink!" And Millie never feared thunder again!

**" . . . don't be afraid. The Lord your God will be with you everywhere you go." (Joshua 1:9, ICB)**

*How did Millie get over her fear of thunder? ______________________

______________________________________________

*What was God's plan? ______________________

______________________________________________

*Do you think God has a plan for everything? ______________________

*What are some of *your* fears? ______________________

______________________________________________

*Do you think God can help you get over your fears? ______________________

Mystery Men
Unscramble the names of these three men. Then use the code below to find out who these mystery men are!
mHa
_ _ _
htpeJha
_ _ _ _ _ _ _
mShe
_ _ _ _
(Genesis 6:10 will help you.)
Code
A B C D E F G H I
J K L M N O P Q R
S T U V W X Y Z

Like a very big umbrella, God's love covers us and protects us! How does His love cover YOU?

Color the umbrella and raindrops. Cut them out. Hang the raindrops from the umbrella points with thread.

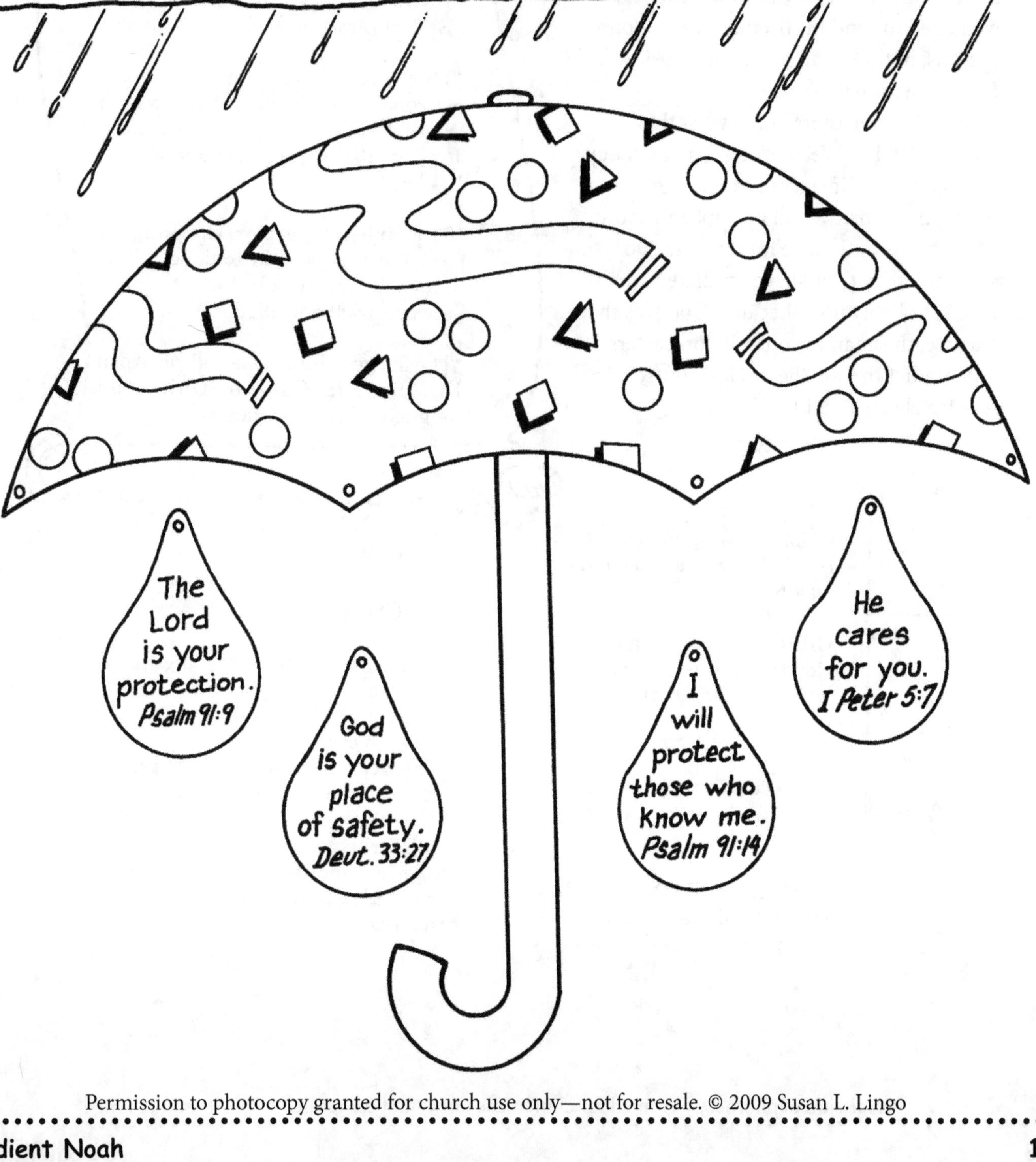

The Lord is your protection. *Psalm 91:9*

God is your place of safety. *Deut. 33:27*

I will protect those who know me. *Psalm 91:14*

He cares for you. *I Peter 5:7*

# Weather Wise

Trying to predict the weather is fun! It's called "forecasting." Benjamin Franklin was one of the earliest forecasters in the United States. He was among the first to notice the patterns of winds and storms and the directions they typically travel. He even tried to send his friends weather predictions, but the mail moved much slower than the weather!

How do forecasters know what the weather will be? Weathermen rely on fancy tools, computer images, and much more to predict if tomorrow will be cool and showery or sunny and made for a picnic. Do you think they could have predicted Noah's flood? Probably not—because God was the chief weatherman in control! Forecasters only predict the weather—God controls it because He created it!

## Did You Know?

*The heaviest rainfall (outside of the Flood!) was in Cherrapunji, India, where they received 1,041 inches of rain in 1 year! (That's almost 87 FEET of rain!)

*The hottest temperature ever recorded in the United States was in Death Valley, California, where, on July 10, 1913, it reached a scorching 134$^{o}$ F!

*The driest spot for the longest period of time was in Iquique, Chile, where no rain fell for 14 years between 1899 and 1913!

*The largest hailstone fell on April 14, 1981, in Canton, Ohio, and weighed in at 30 pounds!

### CLOUDS

CUMULUS—puffy, white, cotton-like clouds; mean nice weather.

CIRRUS—wispy; highest clouds in the sky; mean warmer weather with nice days.

STRATUS—low gray blanket of clouds; mean rain or snow.

THUNDERHEAD—high piles of clouds with a flat base; mean stormy weather soon.

### SKY COLOR

*Red sky in the morning brings a chance of rain.
*Pink sky at night usually means a nice day tomorrow.
*Gray sky in the morning (not gray clouds!) means a nice day ahead.
*Blue, purple and yellow at sunset mean a clear tomorrow.
*Rings around the sun or moon mean coming rain; the bigger the ring, the nearer the rain!

Using your eyes and the weather clues from the last page, try your hand at forecasting! Each morning draw what you think the weather will be like that day—you may wish to use the weather symbols at the bottom of the page. Then at night, in the right-hand side of the box, record what the weather *was like* that day. After a month, look over your chart—you will be surprised at what a good forecaster you are! Just remember—God is the TRUE weatherman! He alone knows what the weather will be, and only God can control the wind and rain, the sunshine and clouds!

| Sunday | Monday | Tuesday | Wednesday | Thursday | Friday | Saturday |
|---|---|---|---|---|---|---|
| Sample: Partly Cloudy / Cloudy and a little rain | | | | | | |
| | | | | | | |
| | | | | | | |
| | | | | | | |
| | | | | | | |

Sunny  Cloudy  Windy  Stormy
Rainy  Snowy

# Do You NO-AH Riddle?

**What game did the rabbits play on the ark?**

Draw straight lines to matching ark animals below. The letters NOT crossed out will spell out the answer!

H O B
E P
S C
V
T A
O D
C H

PUT YOUR ANSWER HERE ___ ___ ___ ___ ___ ___ ___ ___ ___

Answer: Hopscotch

Find the missing words from the verse and fill them in!

"Pairs of clean and unclean _ _ _ _ _ _ _ _ _, all _ _ _ _ _ _ _ _ _ _ _ _ _ that move _ _ _ _ _ the ground, male and _ _ _ _ _ _, came to the _ _ _ _ and entered the _ _ _, as _ _ _ had commanded Noah." (Genesis 7:8, 9)

**WORD BANK**

- creatures
- female
- ark
- animals
- God
- Noah
- along

## What does God give away—yet always keep?

**Color in the boxes with the dots to find the answer!**

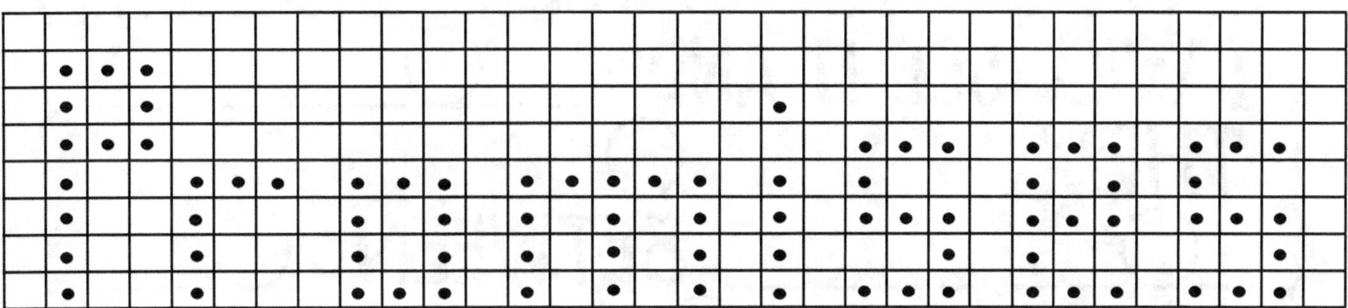

"For the Lord your God will bless you as he has promised."

**Deuteronomy 15:6**

So many valuable things in life must be given away to be kept! Smiles and love are two beautiful gifts that you keep even after you give them away to someone. Can you think of any more?

God's Word is filled with the precious promises He makes to His people. What does God promise us? Read these verses then fill in the blanks to tell what God's promises are!

- Psalm 85:8 ______________________________
- Jeremiah 29: 11 ___________________________
- Genesis 9:11 ____________________________
- Acts 2:33 _______________________________
- Romans 1:2 ______________________________
- Titus 1:2 _______________________________
- James 1:12 ______________________________

# God's Covenant

Look up Genesis 9:16 in your NIV Bible and fill in the missing words below. Then unscramble the circled letters to form two words that will tell you what a COVENANT is.

WHENEVER THE ○_______ ○_______ IN THE __○____, I WILL SEE IT AND __○_____ THE _______○_____ ○________ BETWEEN ○__ AND ALL _○_____ _________○ OF EVERY ___○ ON THE ○_____.

Genesis 9:16

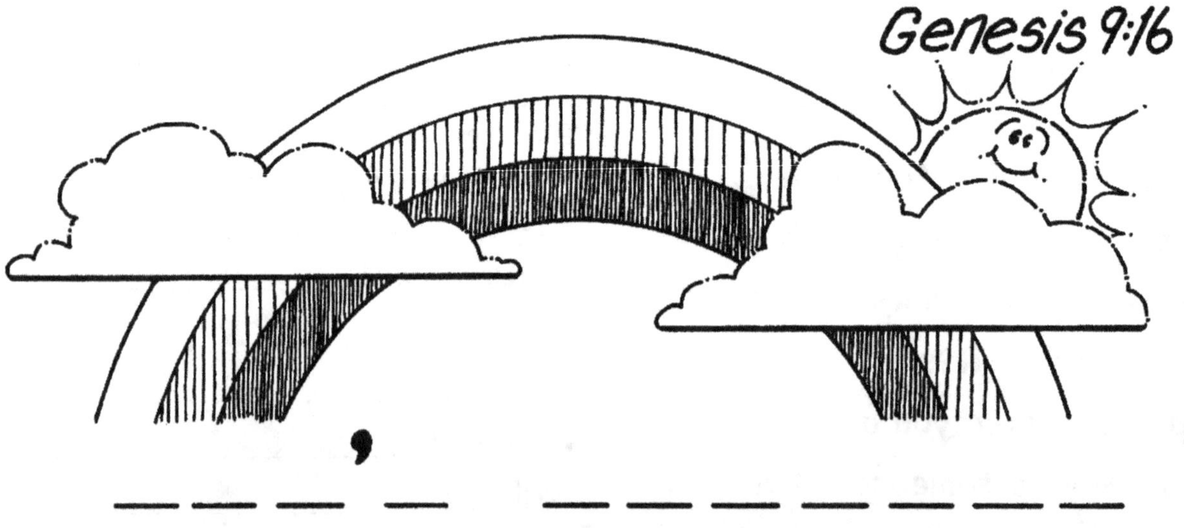

_ _ _ _ _ , _ _ _ _ _ _ _ _ _

# A Pocketful of Promises

## Precious Promise

I have a pocketful of promises
that God has given me—
the wind that tickles tops of trees,
the crashing waves at sea.

He's promised me the rising sun,
the stars and moon when day is done.
His promise kept in birds that sing,
the way that summer follows spring.

Yes, I have a pocketful of promises
that God has given me,
but the most precious pocket promise
is the one that HE'LL LOVE ME!

Make your own pocketful of promises.
1. Trace the pocket; cut two.
2. Tape or glue the sides of the pockets together, leaving the top and the bottom point open.
3. Decorate the top pocket.
4. Color the rainbow, cut it out, and staple it to a craft stick.
5. Insert the stick down through the pocket.

Every time you push the stick upwards, the rainbow will appear as a symbol of God's promises.

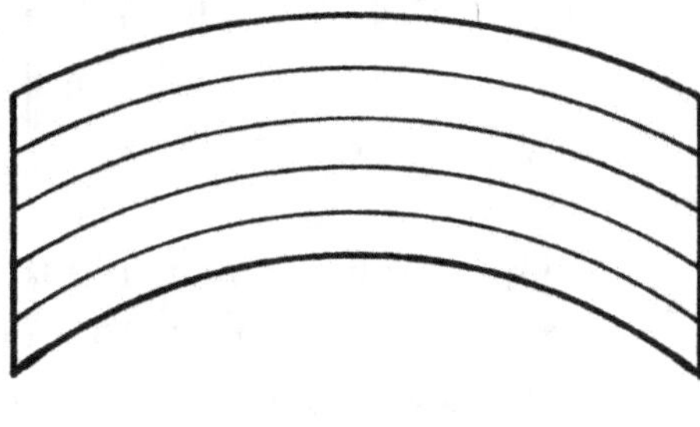

# Rainbow Mobile

The rainbow has come to be a symbol of God's covenant or promise. Make this rainbow mobile and hang it up as a reminder that God always keeps His promises.

**Directions:**

1. Fold a paper plate in half.

2. Glue stretched cotton balls along the edge of both sides and draw a face on each side.

3. Glue tinsel along the inside bottom edge for rain. Staple halves together.

4. Color and cut out a rainbow for the top and tape a piece of yarn or fishing line to the top to hang the mobile in your window!

# Rainbow

From: God
To: You

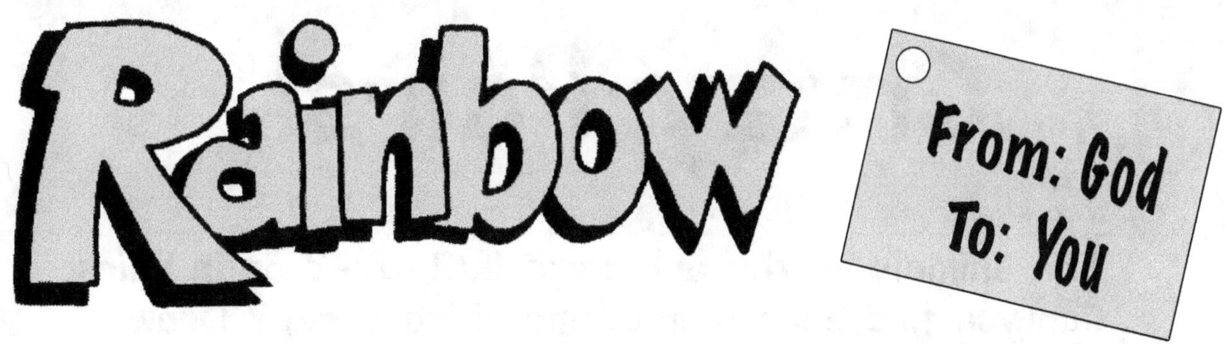

Did you know that another word for "promise" is **covenant?** God made a covenant with Noah and all the world never to kill every living thing again by flood waters. God set a rainbow in the sky as a reminder that His promises are a beautiful sign of His love and Word! Color this rainbow, then learn the verse in the clouds as you remember that God always keeps His promises!

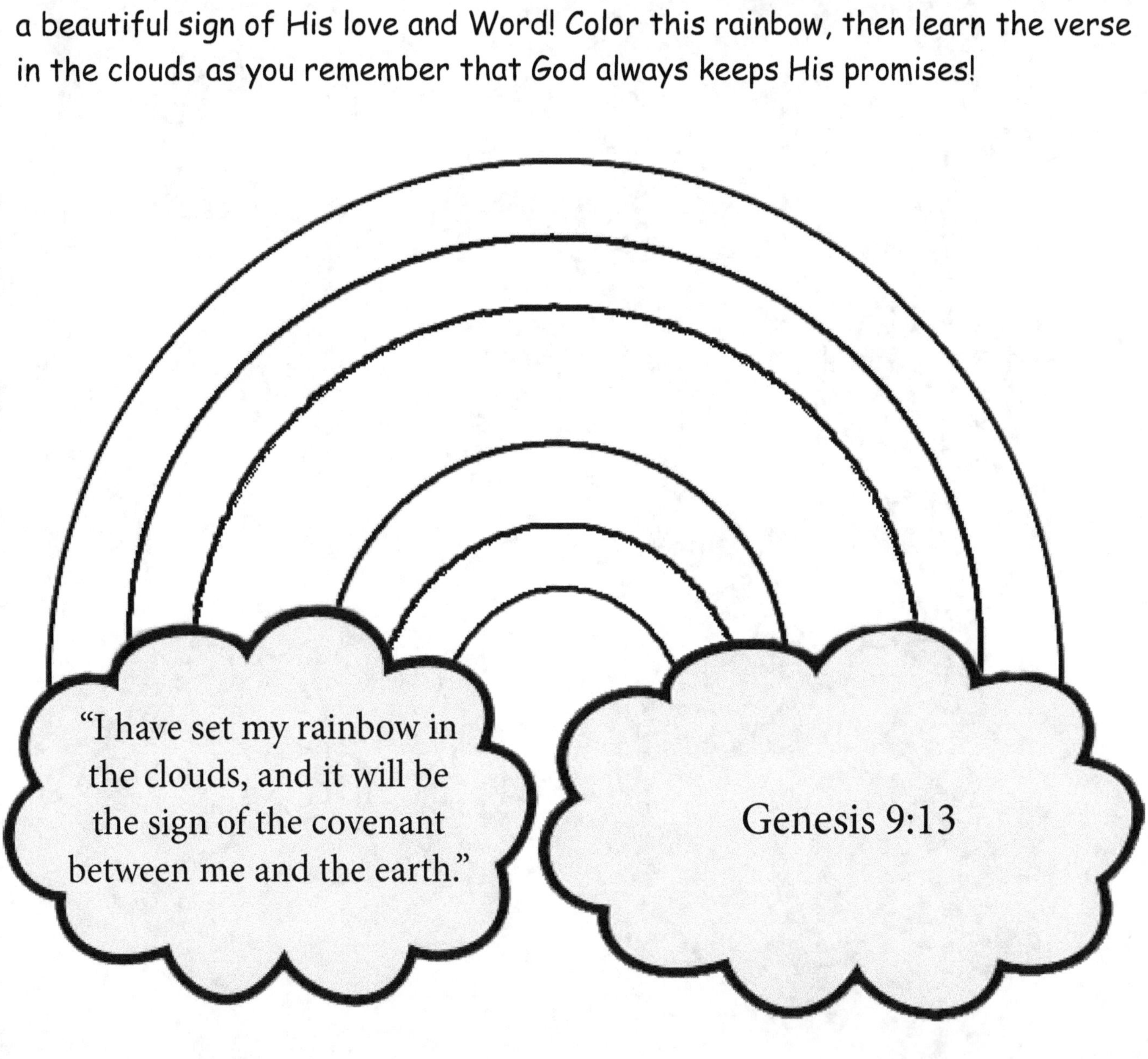
"I have set my rainbow in the clouds, and it will be the sign of the covenant between me and the earth."
Genesis 9:13

# Crazy Pairs!

**The animals on the ark came in 2-by-2 or in pairs. Can you find each pair of matching sheep? Draw lines between the sheep that match.**

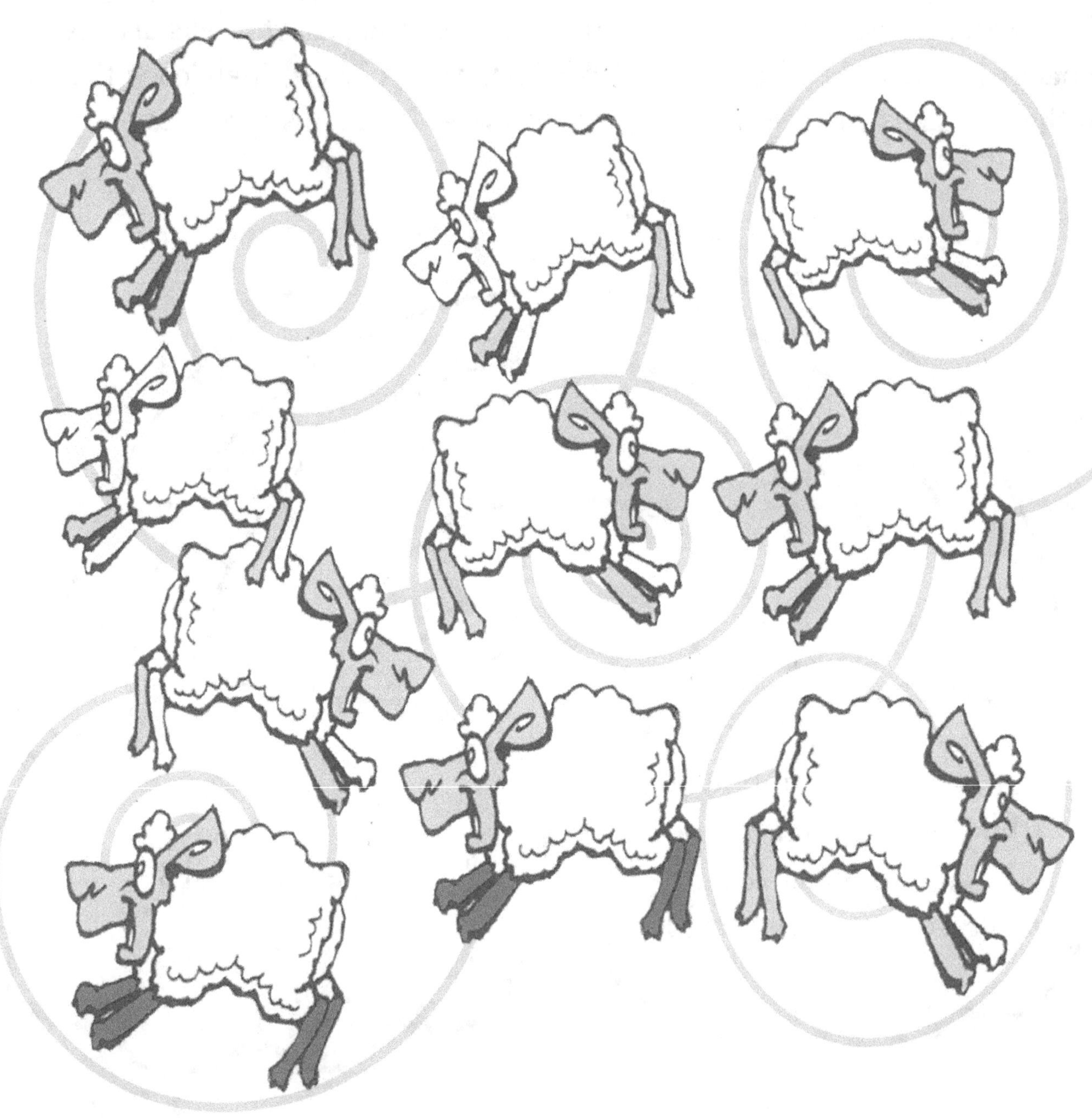

# Obedient Noah

Use your NIV Bible to look up **Genesis 6:22** and fill in the missing words to this memorable memory verse. Then you will discover what Noah always did to honor God in the best of ways! When you're finished, color the picture as you think about how you can obey God in all you do.

"Noah did

__________________

just as

__________

__________________

him."

—Genesis 6:22

**Open any window; open any door.**
**God has given us glorious gifts**
**to seek, to find, to explore!**

God's gift to obedient Noah was His covenant.
Darw a picture of a gift God has given you.

# FAITHFUL ABRAHAM

**"Abraham's faith was credited to him as righteousness."** (Romans 4:9)

In long-ago days, there lived a man named . was a good man and had given his to God. spent his days tending flocks of and loving his wife .

day, the Lord asked to leave his . God said He would lead to the Promised Land. God promised that he would be the father of many ; that would have more than in the sky!

So , , and Abraham's nephew Lot packed up their and their and followed the Lord.

and had no , and this made them feel . God made another promise to and told him that he and would have a . and were old to have a , so just .

But God always keeps His promises! Soon and had a beautiful boy! said, "God has brought me laughter, and everyone who hears about this will laugh with me" (Genesis 21:6). And because God had given and such joy, they named the Isaac, which means laughter!

# Faithful Follower

**"By faith Abraham...obeyed and went, even though he did not know where he was going. By faith he made his home in the promised land like a stranger in a foreign country." (Hebrews 11:8, 9)**

## Blindfolded Following

How do you think Abraham felt being led, not knowing where he was going? Certainly he needed to listen very carefully! If you were in Abraham's place, how hard do you think you would have to listen?

Try this!
You will need a blindfold and a large area with obstacles.

This activity may be done in or out of doors. The object is for the adult leader to guide the blindfolded student through an area in which there are three to four obstacles (going around chairs, under a table, in and out of a large box, etc.). No more than three to four obstacles should be used. The leader should read the following instructions to the students.

1. The student is to pretend to be Abraham.
2. He is to listen carefully to the leader's directions in order to know where to go.
3. He must trust the leader to give him the best directions possible to be successful in completing the journey.

*(Clear, precise directions must be given to guide the student successfully through the area. Students should not see the area before the activity. After all students have completed the course, discuss the experience.)*

1. How did you feel when you didn't know where you were going?
2. Do you think Abraham felt that way?
3. How hard did you have to listen? What happened when you didn't listen well?
4. What did you need to do in addition to listening? (trust the leader)
5. When you went through the activity you could hear the sound of your leader's voice with your ears. How do we hear the directions God gives us? (with our hearts)

To close the activity, read the memory verse again.

Abraham was very special to God—so special that he was called God's friend! Work to memorize the following Scripture verse. Then make Abraham and see if you can lift his arms to give his Father-friend a big hug!

**"Abraham was called God's friend" (James 2:23).**

You need: 4 brads and a craft stick

Directions:

1. Color and cut out pieces.
2. Glue head to the body and attach arms and legs at dots with brads.
3. Staple Abraham to craft stick.

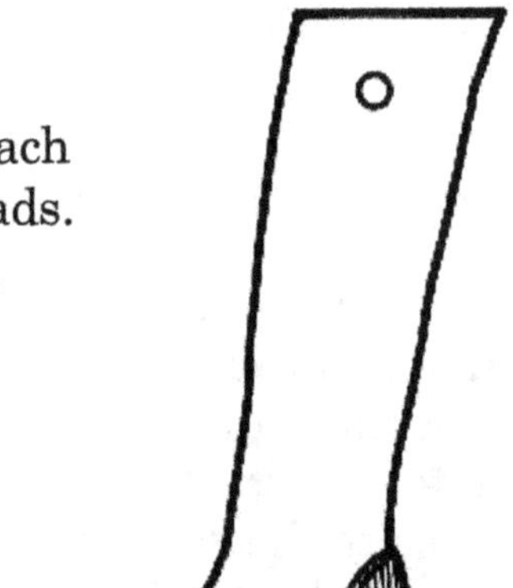

Abraham

God's friend. James 2:23

was

called

# Abraham Gave a "Lot"

Selflessness is placing others' feelings, wants, and needs before our own. It is loving others enough to give them the very best of everything! Read Genesis 13:1-15 (NIV) and then complete the puzzle below to find out how selfless Abraham was.

1. Abraham became very wealthy in _ _ _ _ _ _ _ _ _ _ _ _ . (vs.2)
   13 1

2. Now Lot, who was with Abraham, also had _ _ _ _ _ _ . (vs. 5)
   16

3. But the land could not _ _ _ _ _ _ _ _
   29
   them if they stayed _ _ _ _ _ _ _ _ _ _ _ . (vs. 6)
   5

4. The herdsmen began to _ _ _ _ _ _ _ _ .
   (vs. 7) 22

5. Abraham said to Lot, "Let's not have any quarreling . . . for we are _ _ _ _ _ _ _ _ _ _ _ .
   (vs. 8) 7 18
   Is not the _ _ _ _ _ land before you?" (vs. 9)
   10

6. So Lot chose the green plain of the _ _ _ _ _ _ _ (vs. 11), while Abraham stayed in _ _ _ _ _ _ _ (vs. 12)
   8

7. God saw how selfless Abraham had been, and He gave Abraham all the land he could see for his _ _ _ _ _ _ _ _ _ _ _ forever. (vs. 15)
   3 25

Now arrange the numbered letters in the correct spaces.

God Smiles upon _ _ _ _ _ _ _ _ _ _ _ _ .
16 7 22 3 10 5 1 18 8 13 25 29

# Visitors' Visions

Abraham and Sarah heard about the forthcoming birth of their son Isaac in a wonderous way! Use your Bible (ICB) and read Genesis, chapter 18. Then fill in the missing words below to complete the story of the visit of the three mysterious men!

The Lord ________ (vs.1) to Abraham one hot afternoon. As Abraham looked up, he noticed ______ _____ (vs.2) standing nearby, and he ran to bow _____ (vs.2) before them. Abraham asked them to stay and eat before continuing their _______ (vs.5).

While the three visitors ate, they asked Abraham, "Where is your _____?" (vs.9) He told them Sarah was in their tent. The _____ (vs.10) then spoke and said, "I will _________ (vs.10) return to you about this time a year from now. At that time _____ _____ _____ (vs.10) will have a _____." (vs.10)

Sarah, who was _________ (vs.10) from the tent, _______ (vs.12) at the thought of having a baby now that she was so old! The Lord said to Abraham, "Why did ______ (vs.13) laugh? . . . Is anything too _____ (vs.14) for the Lord? No!"

Sarah was _______ (vs.15) and lied to the Lord saying, "I didn't laugh." But the Lord knew the truth!

Who were these three visitors? Unscramble the highlighted letters in the story to find out!

__ __ __ __ __ __ of the Lord.

# Sarah FLIPS for Isaac

Sarah, unhappy and childless, laughed when God promised her a son. But Sarah soon learned of two great joys: her son, Isaac; and the truth that nothing is too hard for the Lord!

**Directions:**

1. Color, cut, and glue pattern to stiff paper.
2. Tape a tissue to the - - - - - - - line for Sarah's skirt.
3. Make Sarah flip for her precious son, Isaac.

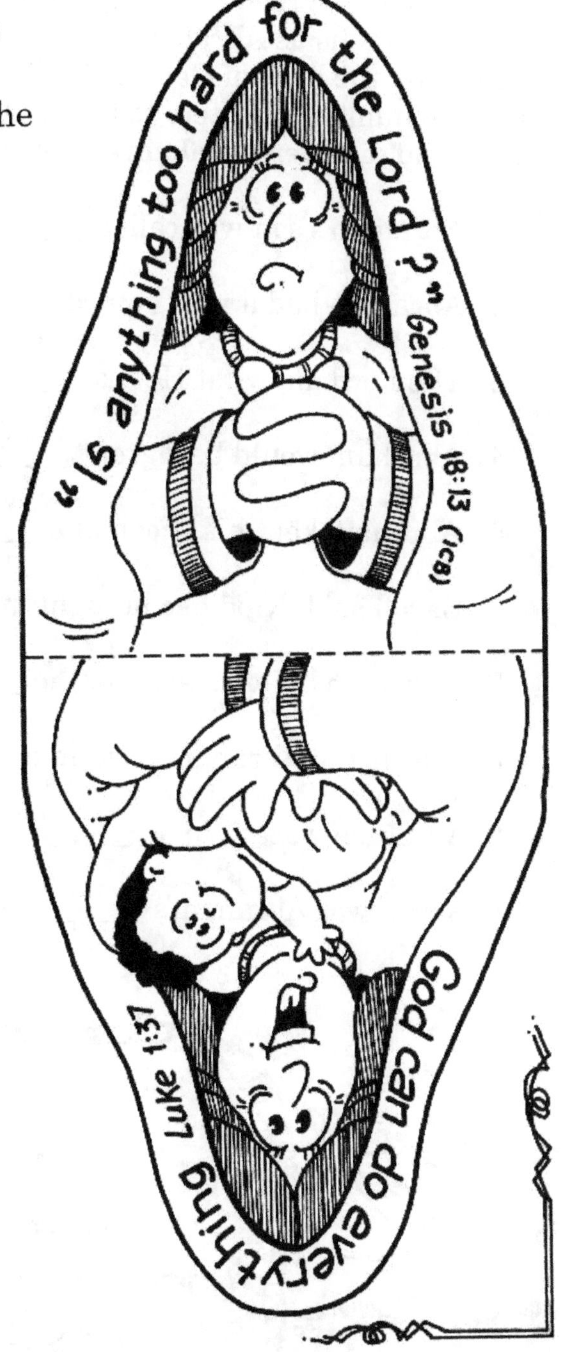

In the Bible we read that Abraham was called the "father of nations." But the Bible also tells us Abraham was called a name even more special. Use your NIV Bible and the book of Genesis to fill in the missing words in the lines below. Then use the numbered letters to fill in the blanks on the stone at the bottom of the page and discover Abraham's special name!

1. Abraham's son was called ___ ___ ___ ___ ___ (21:3).
   8 24 9
2. Abraham had a wife named ___ ___ ___ ___ ___ (17:15).
   10 5 26
3. The Lord did what He had ___ ___ ___ ___ ___ ___ ___ ___ (21:1).
   3 2
4. Abraham would be a great ___ ___ ___ ___ ___ ___ (12:2).
   14 20
5. Abraham kept his sheep in a ___ ___ ___ ___ ___ (21:28).
   1 12 7 16
6. Sarah said, "God has brought me ___ ___ ___ ___ ___ ___ ___ ___ (21:6).
   4 15 13
7. Abraham built an altar to the ___ ___ ___ ___ (12:7).
   23 11 22
8. Sarah and Abraham lived in a ___ ___ ___ ___ (13:18).
   19
9. Abraham was ___ ___ ___ ___ ___ ___ ___ (14:19).
   18 25 17
10. Sarah was Abraham's ___ ___ ___ ___ (18:10).
    6 21

Isaac had to help his father tend their flocks of sheep. Do you suppose that he ever tried to draw them in the sand?

Use a piece of paper and follow the leader!

Draw the sheep on half of a piece of paper. Glue two cotton balls on sheep. Fold the paper in half and stand your sheep up. Can you make a whole flock?

# Family Fun

Are families really different today than long ago? Not so very much. Since the day God created our first mother and father, Adam and Eve, families have felt the Lord's love through our parents, brothers and sisters. And with God as our Abba Father and we His children, we all belong to the wonderfully loving and sharing family of God!

Share some family fun with the two ideas below.

**Family Feelings Board**
Hang a large piece of paper or posterboard on the refrigerator and put markers or crayons nearby. Family members draw or write little messages and pictures on the paper whenever they have a feeling to share. At the end of the day (or week), sit down and share your paper together!

**Family Apple Trees**
Have each person in your family put fingerprint apples on a tree you have colored. (Use red paint or a stamp pad for the apples.) Let each family member draw their face on their apple!

## Did-You-Know?

If you had lived back in the time when Isaac was a child, you'd have called your father "Abba" instead of Dad. You would be living in tents with your grandparents, aunts, uncles, and lots of cousins to work and play with! Your family would be large, because life was not easy and all of the work would need to be shared. With no large grocery stores or department stores to shop for food and clothing, most of your family's days would be spent tending the family flocks of sheep, fixing meals, drawing water from the well, or making clothes from sheep hides.

Then, as today, families shared their work to keep households running smoothly.

Directions for making a family book:

1. Cut out book.
2. Fold on - - - line.
3. Draw pictures for each page.
4. Color your book.

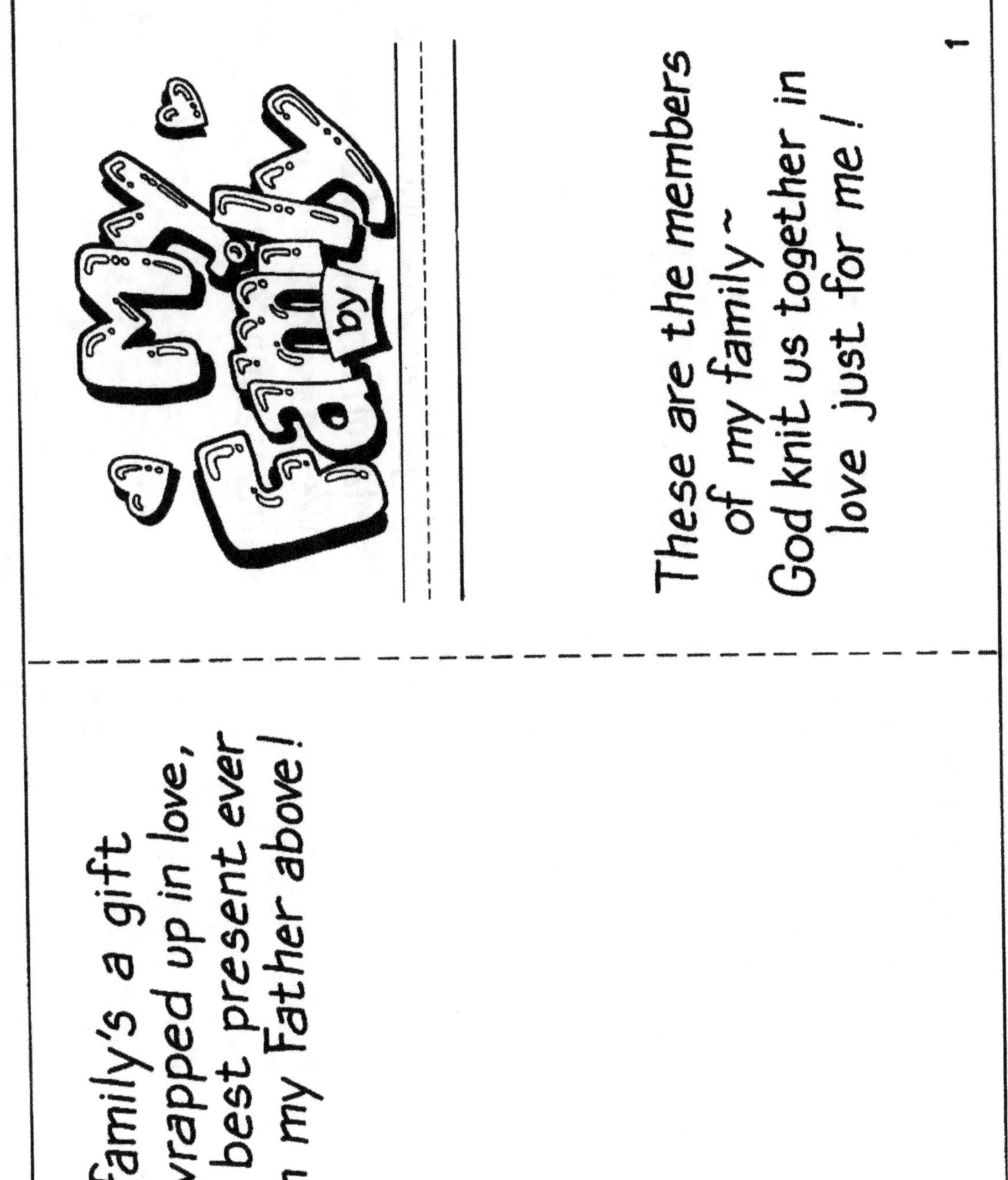

Sometimes we like
to do special things;
here's one of them...
see the smiles that it
brings ?

2

Together we work and we
laugh and we dream.
We share it all 'cuz
my family's a team!

3

# Joyful Creations

## Sheep Necklace

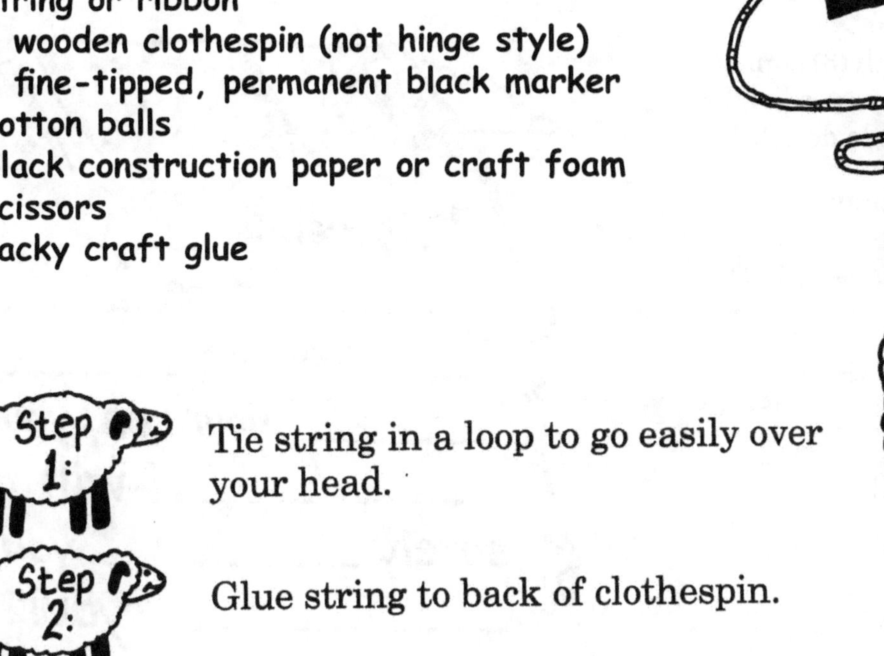

To make each necklace, you'll need:

- string or ribbon
- a wooden clothespin (not hinge style)
- a fine-tipped, permanent black marker
- cotton balls
- black construction paper or craft foam
- scissors
- tacky craft glue

**Step 1:** Tie string in a loop to go easily over your head.

**Step 2:** Glue string to back of clothespin.

**Step 3:** Glue stretched out cotton balls over front and back of clothespin, except over face and bottom of "legs."

**Step 4:** With your marker, color legs and add a face.

**Step 5:** Tear out tiny ears from paper and color them black. Glue them on the sides of the head.

**Step 6:** Let your sheep dry for one day before you wear him!

*"I am the good shepherd; I know my sheep and my sheep know me..."*
*John 10:14*

The poem below tells the story of Abraham's greatest act of faith and obedience. Read the poem and then complete the puzzle using Genesis 22:16, 17 (NIV) and the numbered words in the poem.

Isaac was a gentle one,
Sarah and Abraham's only(3) son.
An obedient child with eyes so bright,
He became Abraham's sole delight!

Then God came to Abraham
To test his belief,
saying, "Climb Mt. Moriah—
return Isaac to me!"

The(5) anguish and pain tore
Abraham apart,
But unfailing faith
was alive in(7) his heart!

The pain flowed so deep,
Yet far deeper still,
Was the faith and(1) the love
to trust in God's will.

He climbed Mt. Moriah
with unfailing trust;
His footsteps a-trudge
In a pathway of dust.

A shiny knife drawn
A tear in his eye,
"I'll love and obey You(2), my God,"
Was his cry.

And God heard his heart,
filled with love and with faith,
And(4) a ram was delivered
To take Isaac's place!

So Abraham learned
Through obedient giving,
Both faith and his son(6)
Were gloriously living!

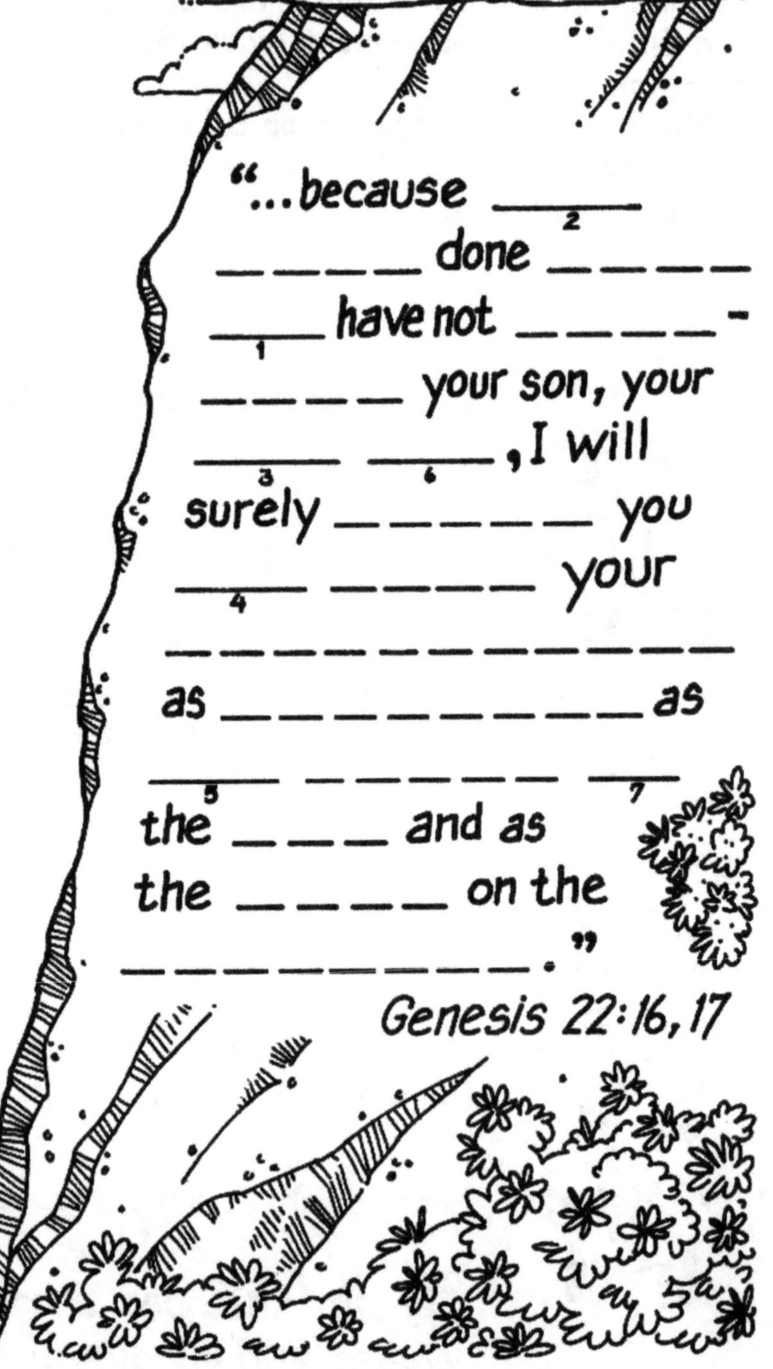

# Mountain Message

**What did Abraham's heart tell him as he climbed the mountain with Isaac?**

(Hint: Look at Proverbs 3:5!)

"

"

...

Find the verse from Hebrews 11:11 (ICB) by traveling along the correct path. Pick up letters as you go and put them on the lines below.

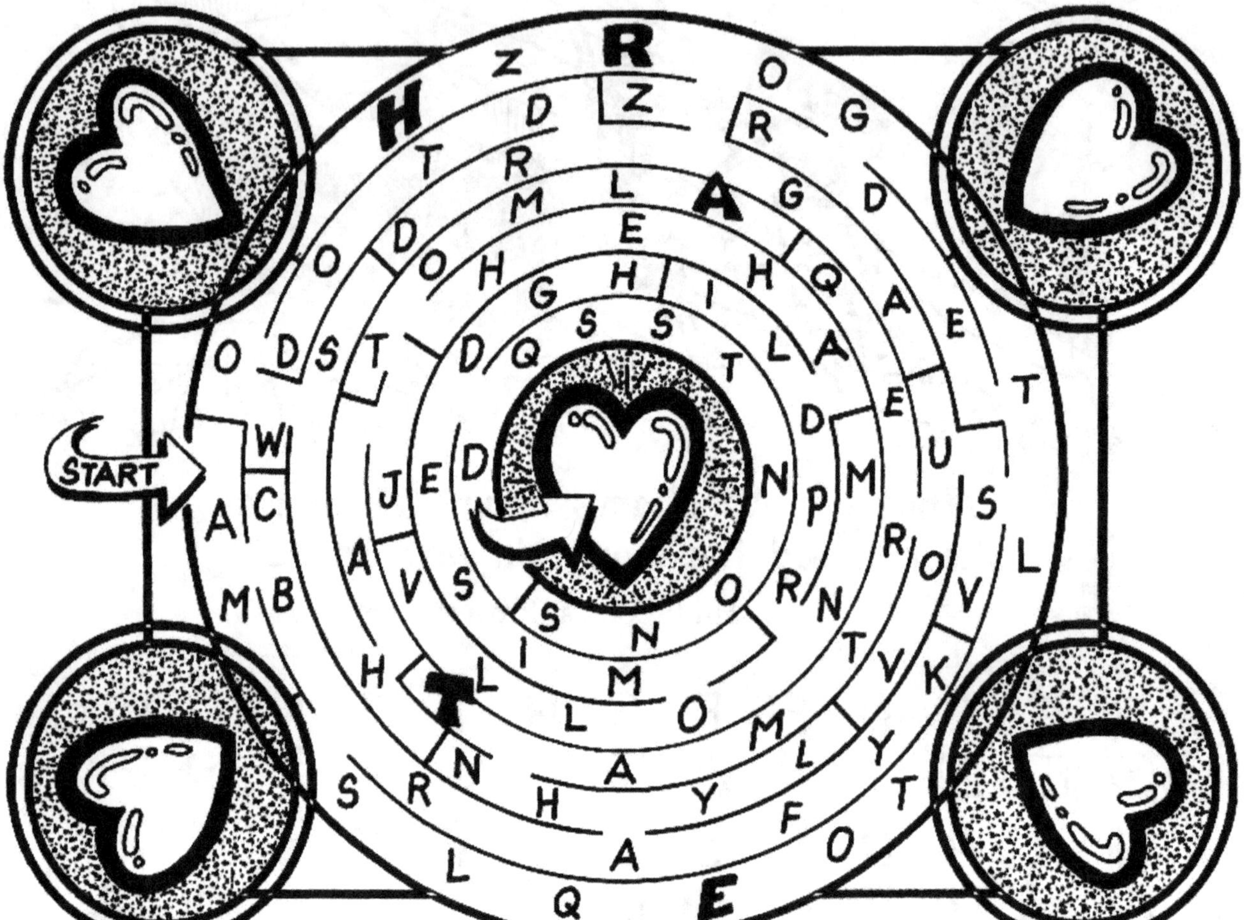

START

______________________________________________

______________________________________________

______________________________________________

Now unscramble the bold faced letters to finish this sentence:

**Abraham trusted God with his whole ___________.**

How small is a whisper? Just that small!
Sometimes it's barely there at all.

It tickles your ear like a summertime breeze—
It's dainty and sweet like a butterfly's sneeze!

As tiny and soft as a hummingbird sings—
Like air that is brushed by angels' wings.

How small is a whisper? Just that small—
Sometimes it's barely...there...at...all.

# Trust Cookies

**INGREDIENTS**

1/2 cup melted butter or margarine
2 cups crushed graham crackers
1 cup flaked coconut
1 package (12 oz.) chocolate chips
1 cup chopped nuts
1 cup sweetened, condensed milk
1 pounf of TRUST

**DIRECTIONS**

1. Layer all of the ingredients IN ORDER in a 9-by-13-inch pan. Do NOT stir! (Trust—remember?)
2. Bake at 325 degrees for 25 minutes or until brown.
3. Cool 10 minutes, then cut into cookie bars and enjoy!

## TRY THIS!

After you make the delicious Trust Cookies, settle kids back as you read them the story of Abraham from a colorful story Bible such as My Good Night Bible. Briefly discuss how faith helped Abraham trust God even when it was hard to do. Remind kids that God wants us to trust Him no matter how hard it may be—and that God will never let us down!

# Faithful Abraham

Use your NIV Bible to look up **Romans 4:9** and fill in the missing words to this memorable memory verse. Then you will discover what helped Abraham continue to obey God even when it was the hardest thing to do! When you're finished, color the picture as you think about how faith and trust help you follow God.

"Abraham's

________________

was

____________________

to him as

____________________."

—Romans 4:9

**Open any window; open any door.
God has given us glorious gifts
to seek, to find, to explore!**

God's gift to Abraham was a listening heart.
Draw a picture of a gift god has given you.

# SERVANT MOSES

"It is the LORD your God you must follow, and him you must revere. Keep his commands and obey him; serve him and hold fast to him." (Deuteronomy 13:3)

# Moses

Once there was a wicked  in Egypt called Pharaoh. The bad  made the  of Israel slaves and wanted every  boy killed. 1 saved her  . She put the  in a  and set it by a  . The  daughter found the  and named him Moses.

When  grew UP, he ran from Egypt. 1 day as he was watching his  , God spoke to him from a burning  . God wanted  to help free the  of Israel.  was very afraid, but he loved God with all his  and obeyed.

told the wicked  that God wanted His  set free. At 1ST the bad  said, "NO!" But God punished the  , and he let  take God's  from Egypt.

and the  followed God's signs to the promised land. In the  they followed a pillar of , and at  they followed a pillar of  . God led His  to safety, and He gave them rules to live by.

and the  thanked God with all their  for His wonderful love!

# Moses, May I ?

**"Observe the commands of the Lord your God, walking in his ways and revering him" Deuteronomy 8:6 (NIV).**

This game is based on the old favorite, "Mother, May I?" Give it a new twist, and you can pretend to be the freed people of Israel trusting Moses to lead your every step from Egypt to the promised land!

1. Choose a player to be Moses. He/she will call the steps. Moses must stand opposite the players (about 20 feet away). Moses is in the promised land.
2. Players line up side by side. The players are in Egypt.
3. Moses will call on one player at a time and tell him how many steps of faith he may take. (Steps are described below.) Example: Take 3 Noah steps.
4. Player must ask: Moses, may I? before he takes his steps. If he forgets to ask, he must go back to Egypt until his next turn.
5. First player to the promised land is the winner and will be Moses for the next game!

## STEPS OF FAITH

ABRAHAM STEP:
Close eyes (and trust!). Take 1 step back and 2 steps forward.

NOAH STEP:
Like the rabbits on the ark, Noah's step is 1 hop!

BABY ISAAC STEP:
Take 1 baby step while laughing.

GOLIATH STEP:
Take 1 giant step.

## Did-You-Know-?

Children of Moses' time played nine pins, a game much like our bowling. They had toys with moving parts, like chariots and wheeled carts, or puppets with arms and legs that moved. Children would go bird hunting with a throw stick (similar to a boomerang). Instead of a dog, they'd use a cat to fetch the birds!

When children were sick, they didn't take aspirin or other medicines that we might use. They might have to take a mixture of boiled beetle and animal fat.

When Pharaoh refused to obey God's command to let the children of Israel leave Egypt, God sent ten plagues upon the Egyptian people. Complete the puzzle to discover what these ten plagues were.

All of the boxes connect with a box containing the same letter. After you finish the puzzle, check your work in Exodus 7—11.

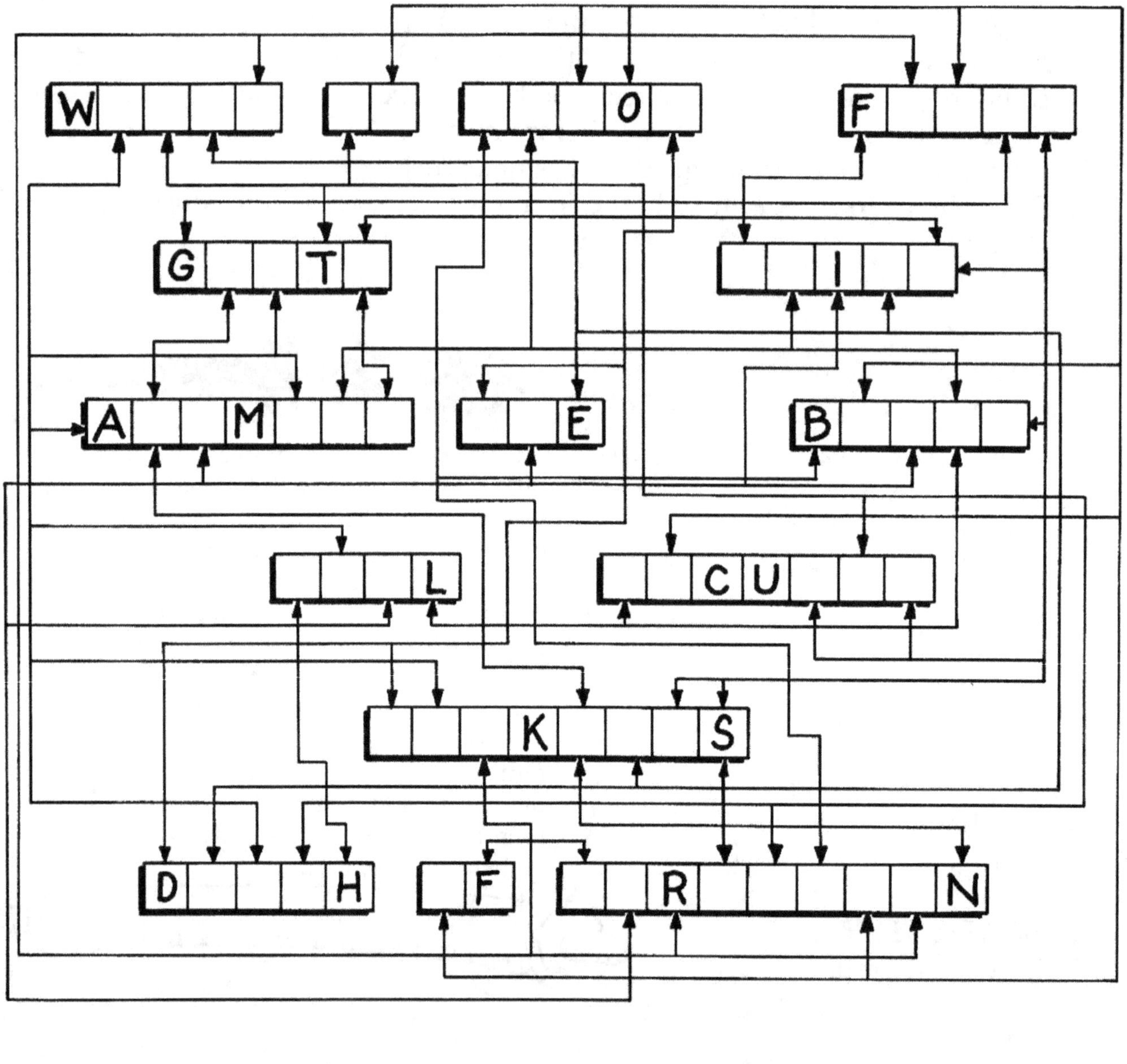

W _ _ _ _    _ _    _ _ _ O _    F _ _ _ _

G _ _ T _    _ _ I _ _

A _ _ M _ _ _    _ _ E    B _ _ _ _

_ _ _ L    _ _ C U _ _ _

_ _ _ K _ _ _ S

D _ _ _ H    _ F    _ _ R _ _ _ _ _ N

# LOCUST LOOK ALIKES

Which three locusts are identical twins?

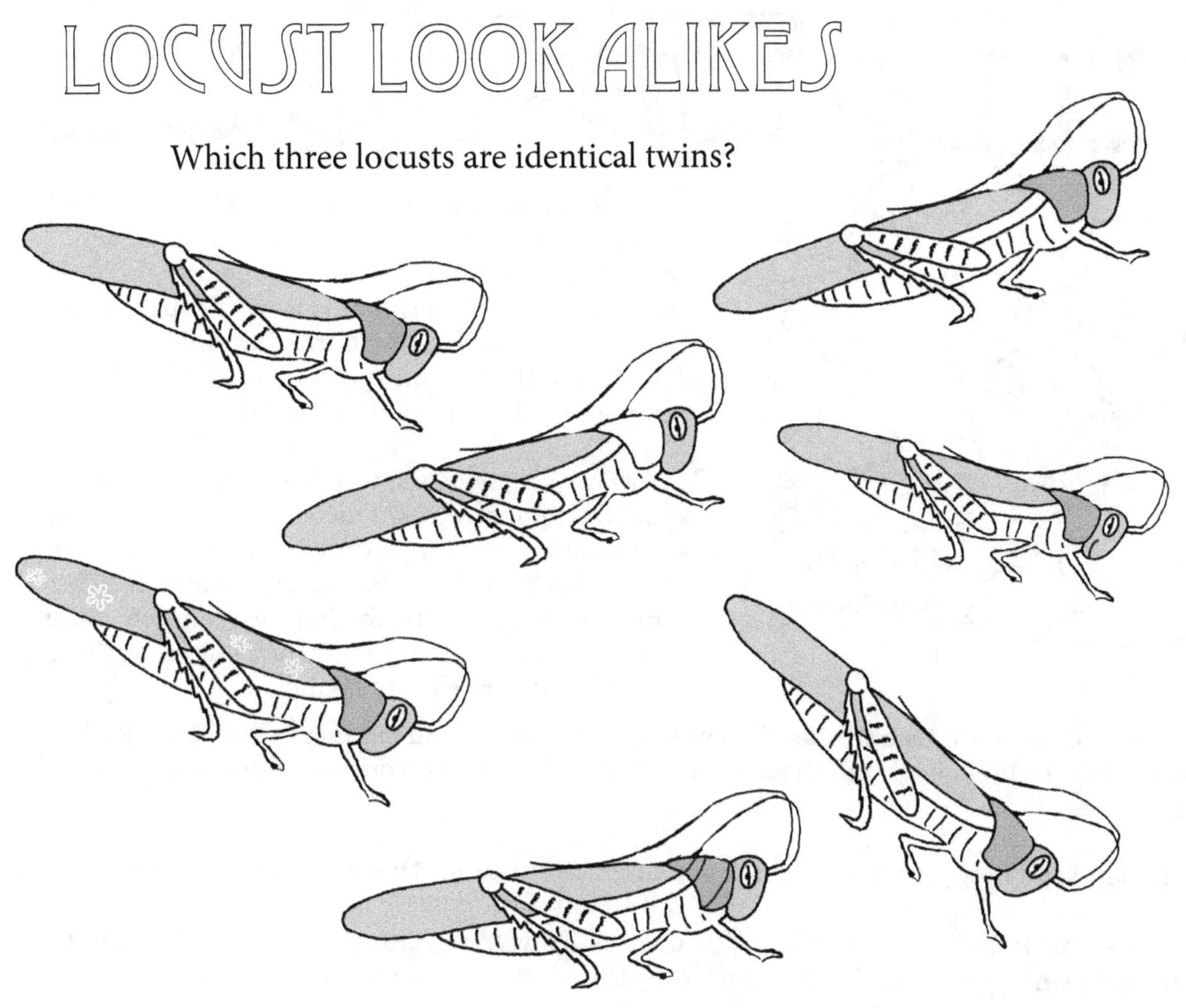

# FRIED LOCUSTS?

In the New Testament, we read about how John the Baptist lived in the wilderness wearing camel hair clothing and a leather belt (Matthew 3:4). But do you know what John the Baptist ate? *Locusts and wild honey!* That's right! Those large, brown locusts were full of nutrition—even if they may not have looked or tasted very yummy fried, boiled, baked, or raw! After all, who likes grasshoppers other than lizards or birds? Ewww!

Try the recipe in the side box for a tasty treat using sweet, stuffed dates as make-believe locusts—and dates were also part of John the Baptist's diet!

**STUFFED LOCUSTS (NOT!)**

YOU'LL NEED:

- pitted, dried dates
- plastic knives
- softened cream cheese
- raisins

HOW TO PREPARE:

1. Gently open the side of a dried, pitted date.
2. Using a plastic knife, stuff the date with soft cream cheese.
3. Cut off small pieces of raisins to use for eyes (stuck in the cream cheese).
4. Enjoy!

# On The Tip of My Tongue

God told Moses to go to Egypt to help His people, but Moses was afraid to go and talk to Pharaoh. He said to God, "I am not a good speaker. I speak slowly and can't find the best words." But the Lord said, "Who made man's mouth? It is I, the Lord. Now go! I will help you speak. I will tell you what to say" (from Exodus 4:10-12, ICB).

How *do* we speak? How are we able to make sounds with our voices? Our voice is able to sound because of air moving in and out of the lungs. This air vibrates over the vocal cords in our neck. The tighter the vocal cords, the higher the pitch of our voice. The more air that is pushed out of our lungs, the louder we are able to sound.

How do we make words and specific sounds? Our brains send signals to our lungs and vocal cords and tongue to tell these parts what to do to form words, sounds, and sentences.

To understand how your voice works, you might want to try these simple experiments:

1. Place your fingers on the middle of your neck. Now hum. Can you feel the vibration in your neck when you hum? This is caused by the air vibrating your vocal cords.

2. Now hum a very low note, then a higher note. Did you feel your neck move? This was your vocal cords loosening and tightening to make different sounds.

Because Moses felt tongue-tied, Aaron, his brother, spoke for Moses before the people. Try twisting and tying *your* tongue tightly with these tough tongue twisters!

- ☐ God's great grace gave good gifts!
- ☐ Pharaoh finally felt fear!
- ☐ Moses munched much manna in the morning.
- ☐ Live and love the Lord's laws.
- ☐ The Red Sea saw six slaves slip and slide!
- ☐ God made many mighty miracles!

"My tongue will speak of your righteousness and of your praises all day long." (Psalm 35:28)

# "CAN"fidence

*"I can't do it!"* cried John one day;
he didn't think he could.
*"I just can't DO it!"* they heard him say;
he didn't think he would!

John never thought he'd do it right
and so he never tried.
He said, *"I CAN'T!"* both day and night;
he pouted, fussed, and cried.

But there was One who knew John could,
who said, **"Oh, yes you CAN!"**
He said, **"Have faith, dear John, you should
lean on my helping hand!"**

And so John put his faith in Him
and for the first time tried!
John's heart believed and leaned on Him;
*"I CAN! I CAN!"* John cried.

**✔ TRY THIS!**

Ask kids to tell about times they may have been afraid, frustrated, or sure they couldn't do something. Remind kids that we all feel this way and want to rely on Jesus to help and strengthen us evey day!

* Why didn't John even try to do anything?
* Who was the One who said to John, "Oh, yes you can!"?
* What can *you* do next time you want to say, "I can't!"?

The poem "CAN"fidence may be read in parts by teachers or older children for some extra fun! John's part is in italics, the narrator's part in standard print, and God's voice is in bold print. Make a simple puppet of John by following the directions below.

1. Color and cut out two faces for John—a sad face and a happy face.
2. Glue or staple faces on either side of a craft stick.
3. Show John's sad face during the reading of the poem, until you reach the last line—then show his happy face.

"I can do everything through him who gives me strength." (Philippians 4:13)

Photocopy and color this 2-page game board. Glue to a sheet of poster board or an open file folder to play again and again!

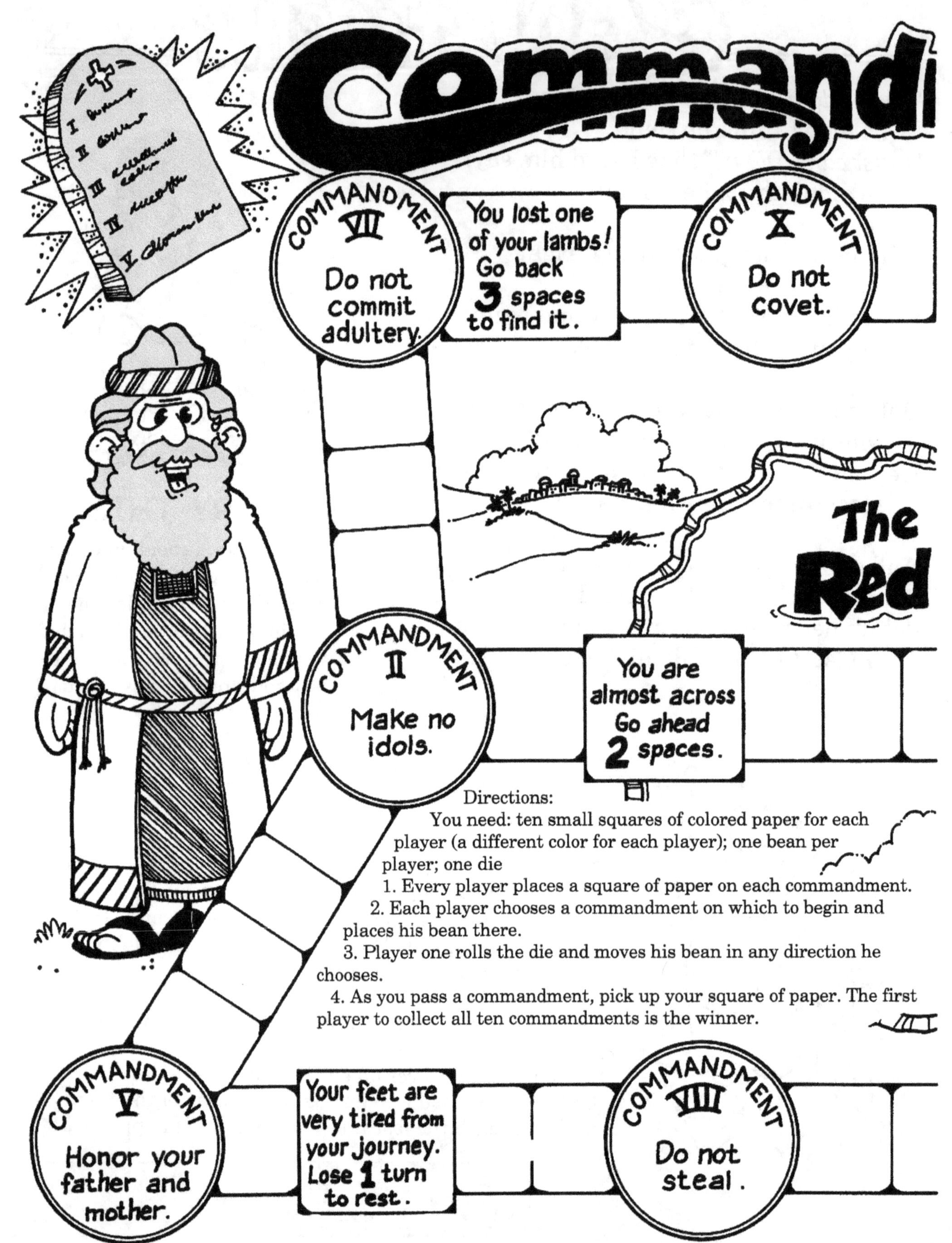


Directions:

You need: ten small squares of colored paper for each player (a different color for each player); one bean per player; one die

1. Every player places a square of paper on each commandment.
2. Each player chooses a commandment on which to begin and places his bean there.
3. Player one rolls the die and moves his bean in any direction he chooses.
4. As you pass a commandment, pick up your square of paper. The first player to collect all ten commandments is the winner.

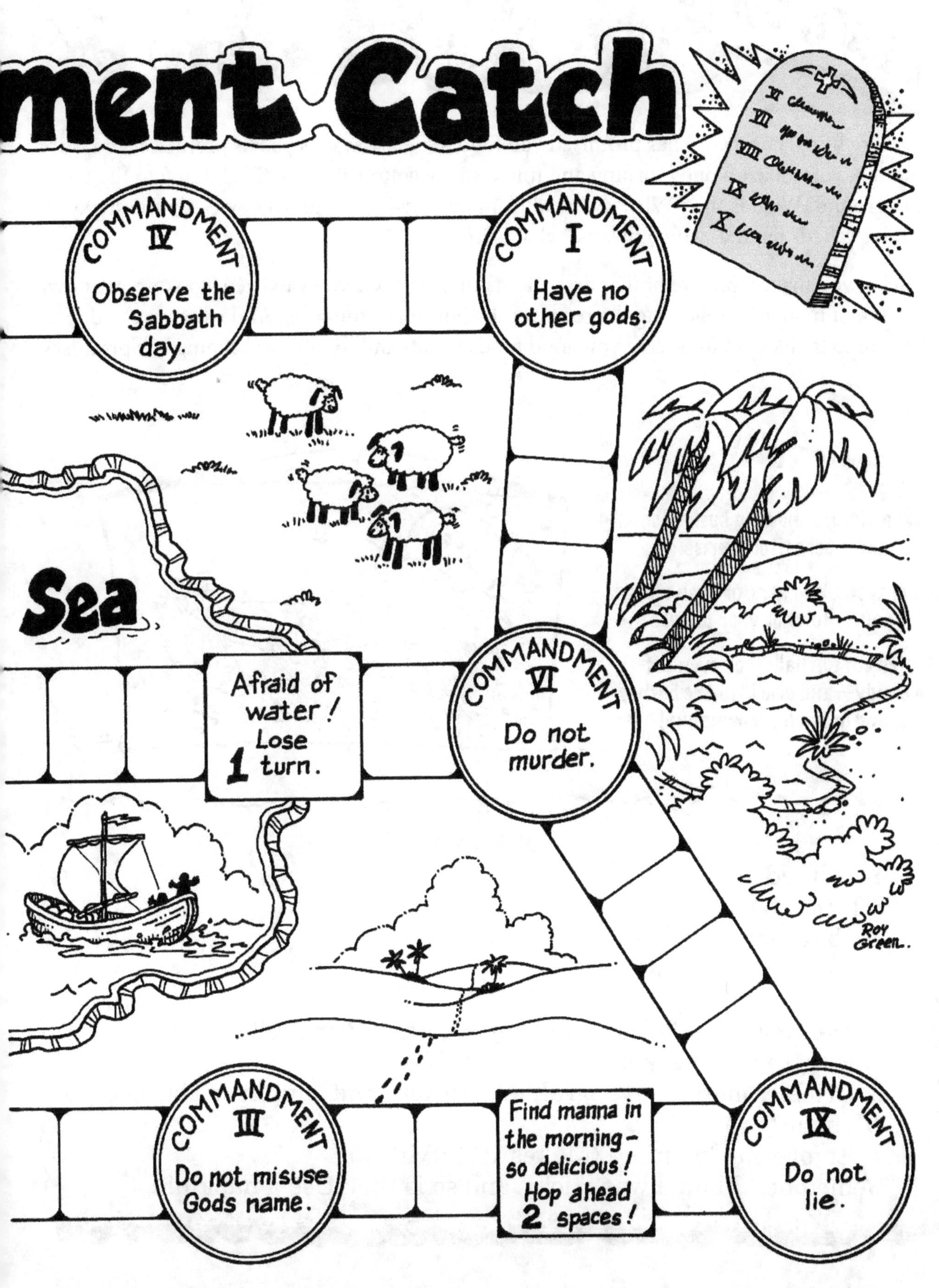
ment Catch
COMMANDMENT IV
Observe the Sabbath day.
COMMANDMENT I
Have no other gods.
Sea
Afraid of water! Lose 1 turn.
COMMANDMENT VI
Do not murder.
ROY GREEN.
COMMANDMENT III
Do not misuse Gods name.
Find manna in the morning - so delicious! Hop ahead 2 spaces!
COMMANDMENT IX
Do not lie.

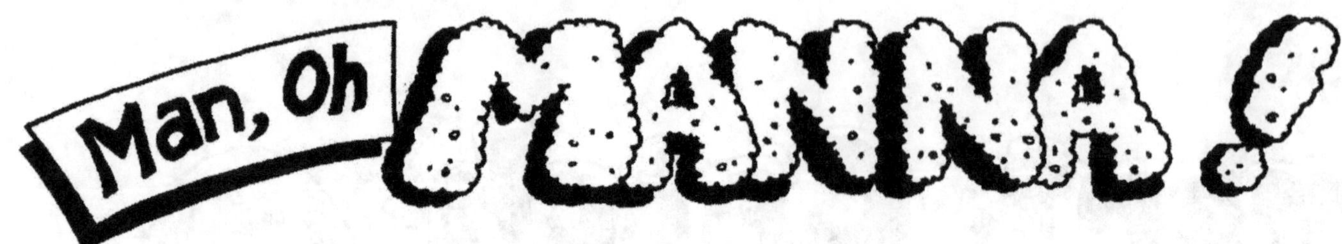


You're hungry and God has promised you food. God always keeps His promises, and, sure enough, you wake up one morning and find a sticky cotton-like "stuff" clinging to the bushes and ground. What is this? Why, it's bread from heaven—given to you by God! The sticky food is called "manna" which means "what is it?"

See if you make a picture of that first manna morning. Or you can even cook up your own version of manna by following the recipe at the bottom of the page. And when you're done, be sure to thank God for giving you good foods to eat–and for always keeping His promises!

## TRY THIS!

1. Draw a picture showing bushes, small trees, and a beautiful sunrise.
2. Use crayons, markers, or even water color paints to color your picture.
3. Stretch cotton balls—or even cotton candy—and glue it to the bushes, trees, and ground. Mmmmanna!

### MANNA

**You need:**
3 T honey
1/2 bag marshmallows
10 graham crackers

1. Melt marshmallows and honey together. Stir well!
2. Put graham crackers on a cookie sheet.
3. Dribble "manna" over graham crackers and chill in refrigerator 1/2 hour (or more).
4. Enjoy your "manna"! (Makes 10 servings.)

Remember! Manna was sticky, and so is this. Use a napkin!

God showed His chosen people amazing grace when he used Moses to lead them out of Egypt and on to the Promised Land!

See if you can find the path from Egypt to the Promised Land in the maze below.

EGYPT

Honey

Milk

Promised Land

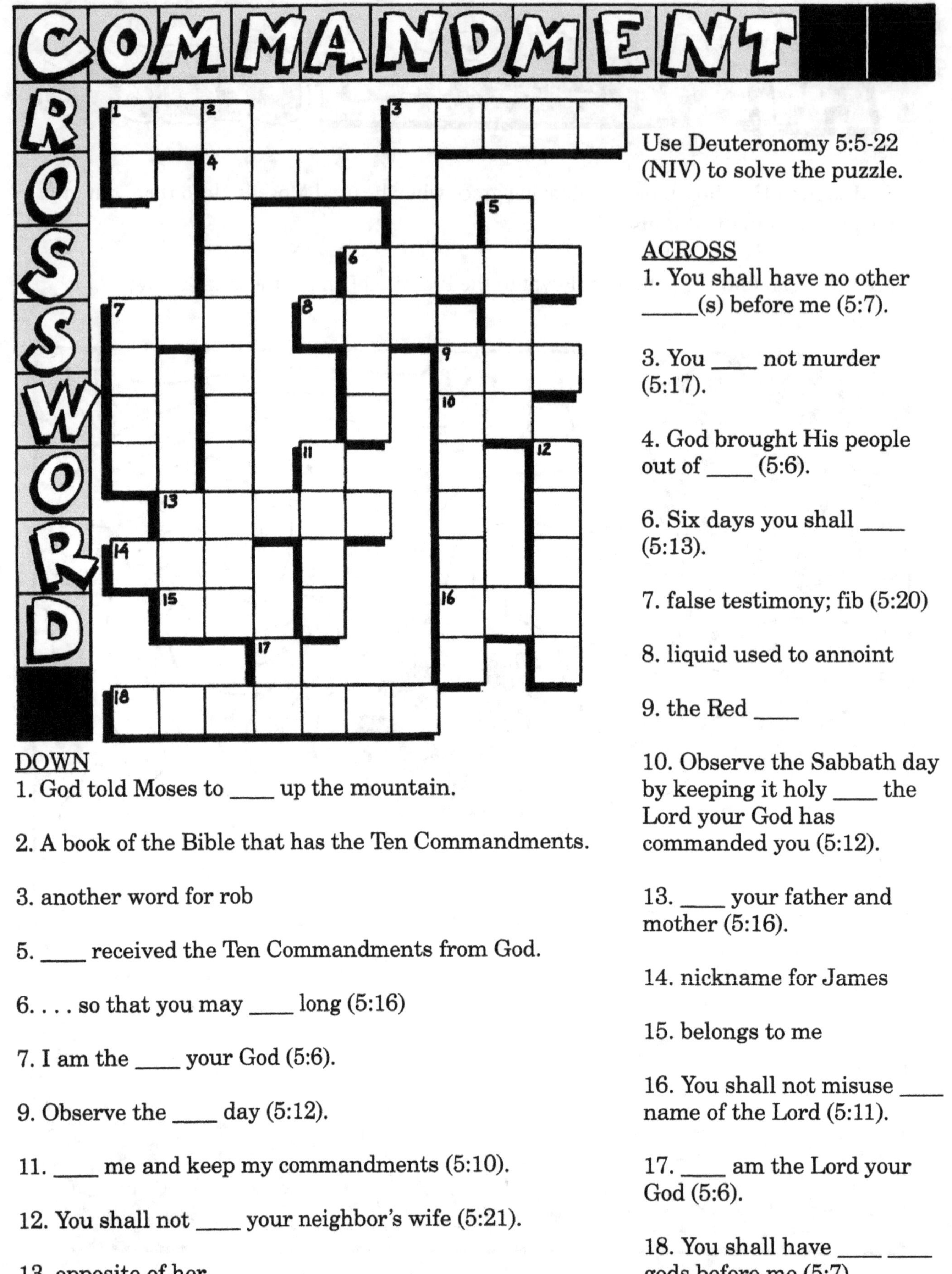


Use Deuteronomy 5:5-22 (NIV) to solve the puzzle.

ACROSS

1. You shall have no other _____(s) before me (5:7).

3. You ____ not murder (5:17).

4. God brought His people out of ____ (5:6).

6. Six days you shall ____ (5:13).

7. false testimony; fib (5:20)

8. liquid used to annoint

9. the Red ____

10. Observe the Sabbath day by keeping it holy ____ the Lord your God has commanded you (5:12).

13. ____ your father and mother (5:16).

14. nickname for James

15. belongs to me

16. You shall not misuse ____ name of the Lord (5:11).

17. ____ am the Lord your God (5:6).

18. You shall have ____ ____ gods before me (5:7).

DOWN

1. God told Moses to ____ up the mountain.

2. A book of the Bible that has the Ten Commandments.

3. another word for rob

5. ____ received the Ten Commandments from God.

6. . . . so that you may ____ long (5:16)

7. I am the ____ your God (5:6).

9. Observe the ____ day (5:12).

11. ____ me and keep my commandments (5:10).

12. You shall not ____ your neighbor's wife (5:21).

13. opposite of her

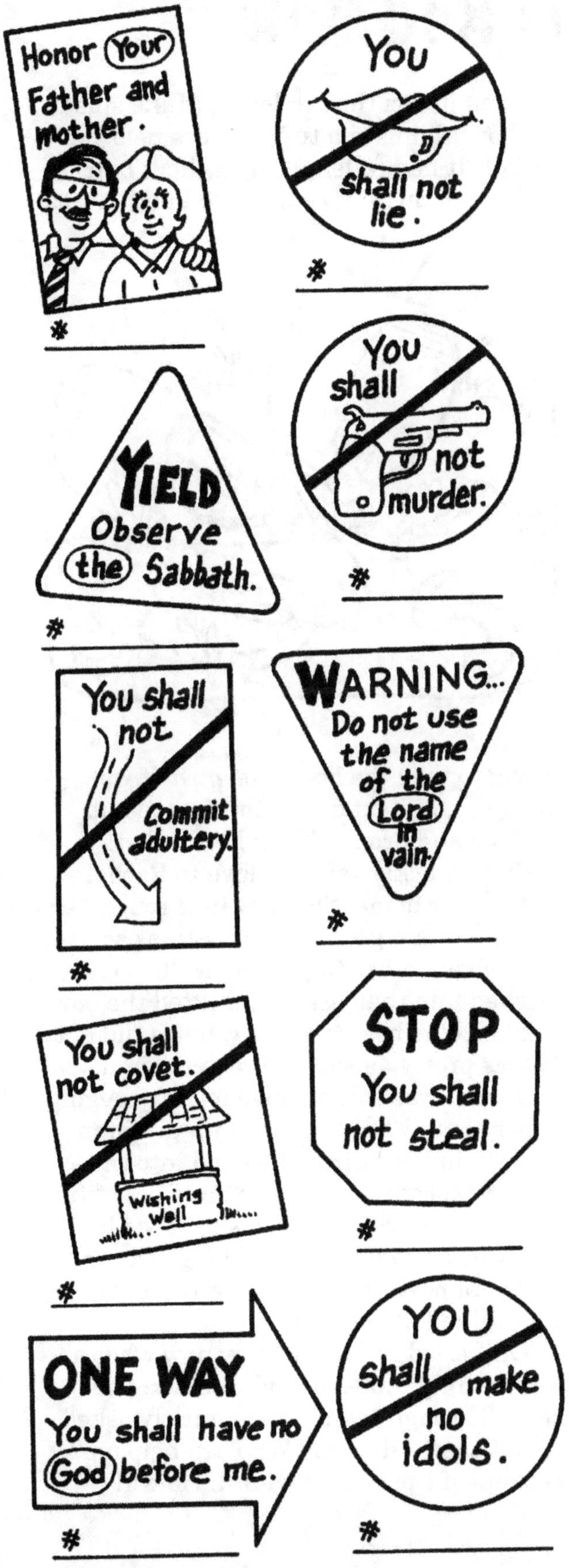

Honor (Your) Father and Mother.

# ________

You shall not lie.

# ________

YIELD
Observe (the) Sabbath.

# ________

You shall not murder.

# ________

You shall not commit adultery.

# ________

WARNING...
Do not use the name of the (Lord) in vain.

# ________

You shall not covet.

Wishing Well

# ________

STOP
You shall not steal.

# ________

ONE WAY
You shall have no (God) before me.

# ________

YOU shall make no idols.

# ________

STOP and

CLEAN YOUR ROOM UP, PLEASE!
LOOK both ways when you cross the street;
Cover your mouth when you Sneeze.
ENTER EXIT

street;
Wash your hands before you eat.
Railroad crossing—
Please go S-L-O-W.
Don't talk to people you don't know!

Sometimes it seems too many
rules are what the world's
made of,
But rules are made to
keep us safe and show us
we are loved!

Just as street signs are made to keep us safe, so God's commandments are like heavenly signs—protecting, teaching, and showing us how we are to live. Use Deuteronomy 5 to number the commandments 1-10 in their correct order. Then unscramble the circled words in the signs to complete the greatest commandment of all.

"Love _____ ________ your ______ with all ________ heart." (Mark 12:30)

# Millie and the Red Bow

Millie Mouse was singing as she packed her tiny picnic basket. Her eyes were bright with excitement as she nibbled a wee bit of cheese before wrapping it up tightly. Millie was going on a picnic with her best friend, Rachel Rabbit.

The sunny afternoon stretched out before Millie like a shiny promise as she skipped across the meadow to Rachel's house. Rachel was already outside waiting for Millie. The first thing Millie noticed about Rachel was the beautiful bow in her hair! It was as red as any cherry she had ever seen. It was fluffy and shiny and it was tied in big loops! In that moment, Millie couldn't think of anything in the world she wanted more than that beautiful red bow!

Millie and Rachel skipped to their favorite picnic spot under the tall oak tree on the hill behind Rachel's hutch. Their picnic blanket billowed in the wind and settled on the grass as they spread it out for their lunch of cheese bits and carrot crisps that Millie had brought and the chocolate cake that Rachel had baked for Millie. And all the while, Millie could not stop watching and wanting the beautiful bow perched on Rachel's head!

When it was time to leave, Millie spied the bow hiding in a tuft of grass near her basket. It had fallen from Rachel's hair and she hadn't noticed! Millie knew it was

wrong to take the bow; she *knew* it was wrong . . . but suddenly, she scooped up the bow and dropped it in her basket!

Millie quickly said goodbye to Rachel and ran for home. She flew in through her front door and gasped for breath as she set the basket on her tiny table. Millie gently reached into the basket and lifted the bow to admire its beauty. Funny, but it did not look as pretty as she had remembered. And what was this strange feeling tugging at her tummy? She reached up to fasten the bow in her hair and looked into the mirror expecting to see the most beautiful bow in the world. Instead, she saw a bow that was dull and sadly sagging. The once-beautiful bow wasn't pretty any longer, and Millie felt sick inside.

"Oh!" cried Millie, "I know now what a wrong thing I have done!" She hung her head. Through tears, Millie quietly asked, "What shall I do now? Who can help me? Perhaps if I pray to the Lord, He will speak to my heart and tell me what to do." Millie, a small gray ball of unhappiness, bowed her head and prayed.

Almost at once, her heart began to speak to her! In that instant, Millie knew why God tells us not to steal! Because of His great love for us, He knows that stealing hurts not only others but ourselves as well. Millie knew what she must do and scampered, with the bow, to Rachel's house.

Rachel came to the door in tears. "Millie, I cannot find my favorite bow anywhere. I must have lost it on our picnic!" Millie gulped. God was right; stealing *does* hurt. Both she and Rachel were hurting!

Millie took a deep breath and handed Rachel the bow. "R-r-rachel, I took your bow. It was so pretty that I wanted it for myself. I was wrong, and I am so sorry! Will you forgive me? Are we still best friends?"

Rachel's eyes filled with sunshine and she forgave Millie. They were still best of friends! Millie's heart swelled with love for her very best friend who loved her enough to speak to her heart . . . God!

♥ How did Millie feel when she did something she knew was wrong?

♥ How did praying help Millie? When do you go to God in prayer?

♥ What did Millie learn about stealing and about God's great love for her?

♥ Have you ever forgiven anybody or have you ever been forgiven? Tell about how you felt.

**"You shall not steal." Deuteronomy 5:19**

# God's Word

Have you ever felt alone or afraid and wanted someone you love close to you? God has promised to always be with us—we are *never* alone!

Memorize the following verse, and then make the Heart of God necklace described below. Wear it close to your heart to remember that God is forever near.

**"God said, 'I will be with you'" Exodus 3:12 (ICB)**

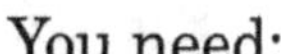

You need:

*pre-cut wooden heart (from craft store) or use the pattern below to cut a heart from a plastic milk jug
*red markers or paint
*ribbons, buttons, glitter, etc. for decoration
*yarn or fishing line
*paper punch

Use the markers or paint and other items to decorate your heart. Glue a piece of paper with the Scripture from Exodus 3:12 printed on it to the center of the heart. Punch a hole in the top center of the heart. Cut a piece of yarn or fishing line long enough to go over your head and hang loosely around your neck. Thread the yarn through the hole and tie it. Allow your necklace to dry before wearing it.

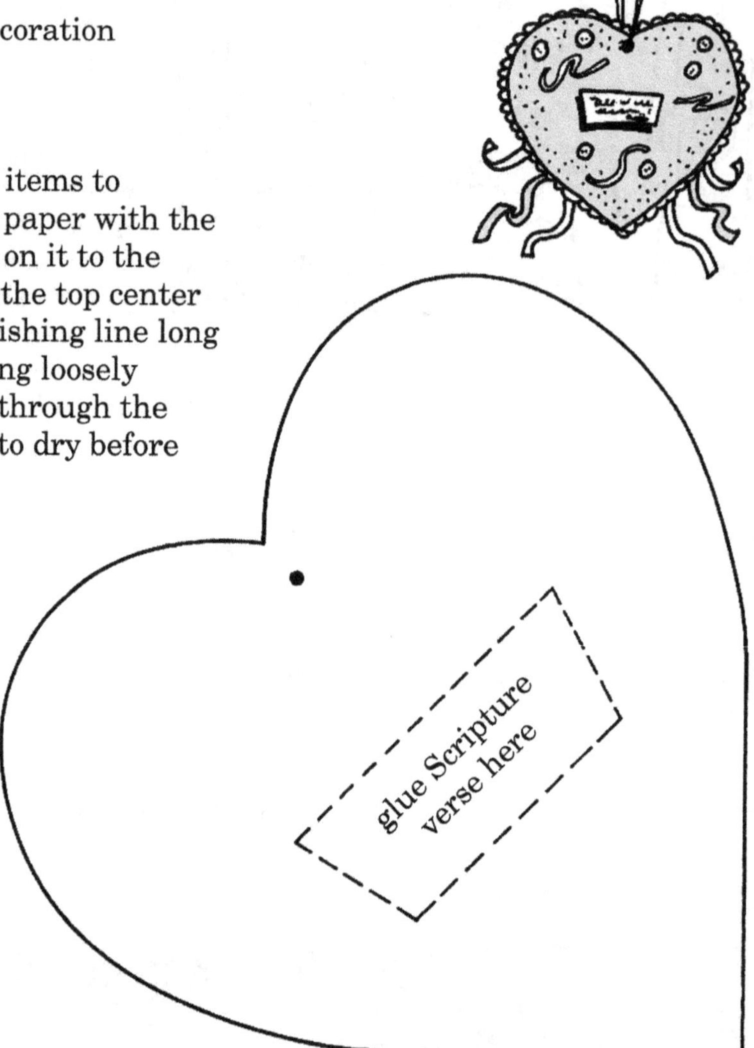


"God said, 'I will be with you.'"
*Exodus 3:12*

# Commandment MATCH UP

1. Cut out cards and mix them up.
2. Place cards face down in four rows.
3. The first player turns over two cards. If they match (commandment with its correct number), he keeps the pair. If they do not match, he turns them back over and the next player takes his turn.
4. The player with the most matched sets is the winner!

(Teacher: You may wish to photocopy this page before cutting it apart so you will have a ready list of the commandments and their chronological number.)

| Commandment I | Commandment III | Commandment V | Commandment VII | Commandment IX |
|---|---|---|---|---|
| You shall have no other gods before me. | You shall not misuse the name of the Lord. | Honor your father and mother. | You shall not commit adultery. | You shall not give false testimony. |
| Commandment II | Commandment IV | Commandment VI | Commandment VIII | Commandment X |
| You shall not make for yourself an idol. | Observe the Sabbath day by keeping it holy. | You shall not murder. | You shall not steal. | You shall not covet. |

# Seek and You Shall Find

The words below are all a part of the story of Moses. See if you can find them in the box at the bottom of this page!

| | | |
|---|---|---|
| Moses | Mt. Horeb | leader |
| Egypt | Miriam | staff |
| locust | chosen | Pharaoh |
| trust | commandments | promised land |
| Aaron | Red Sea | burning bush |

# Servant Moses

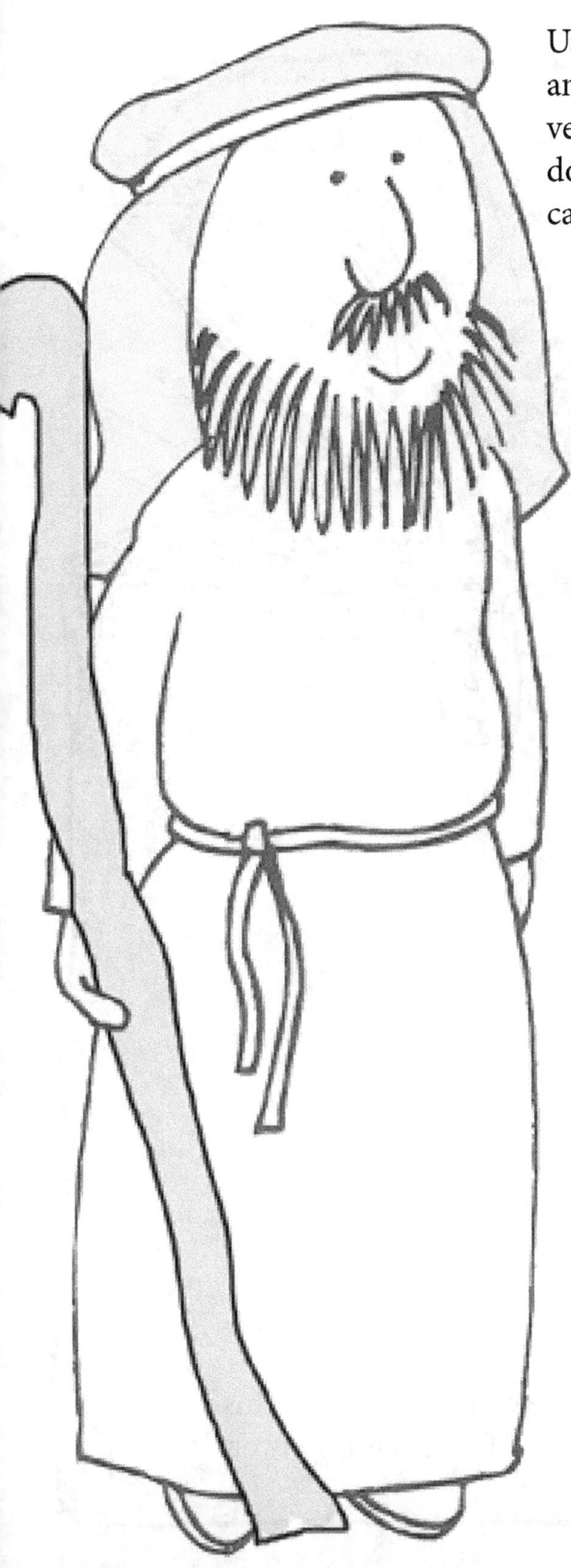

Use your NIV Bible to look up **Deuteronomy 13:4** and fill in the missing words to this awesome memory verse to discover what Moses always remembered to do. Then color the picture as you think about show you can obey God's Word, too!

"It is the _____ your God you must ______, and him you must _______. Keep his ________ and ______ him; serve him and hold fast to him."

—Deuteronomy 13:4

**Open any window; open any door.**
**God has given us glorious gifts**
**to seek, to find, to explore!**

God's gift to Moses was the confidence to lead his pepole. Draw a picture of a gift god has given you.

# LOYAL JOSHUA

**"Choose for yourselves this day whom you will serve....But as for me and my household, we will serve the Lord."**

(Joshua 24:15)

# Joshua Leads God's People

 Joshua

 Jericho

 Rahab

 Soldiers

After Moses died on the of Nebo, God came to and told him lead the of Israel in the promised land. God told to be strong of and keep His laws and the Ten . God promised that if he held God's laws in his , that God would always be with him!

The city of was like a to the promised land, but the of were not God's . would have to fight the of to get to the promised land of Canaan.

 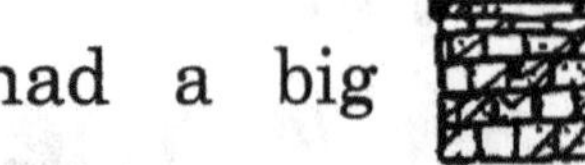 had a big  around it, so  sent  spies to 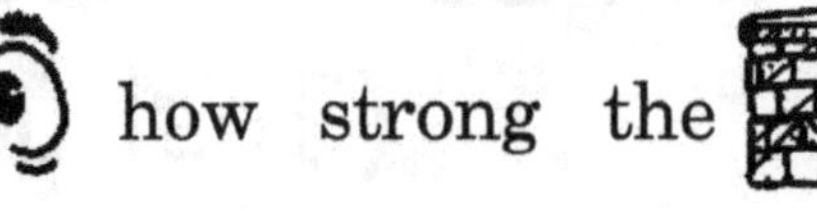 how strong the 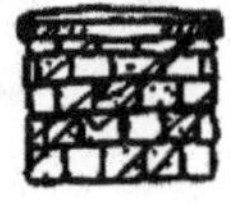 was. The spies met ,

a woman who feared God in her  . She helped the  spies, and they promised that  and her family would be safe.  tied a red  to her  so  and his  would know who to save.

An  with a  told  how God would give  to his  .  listened with his  S and  and obeyed God. God's  walked around the 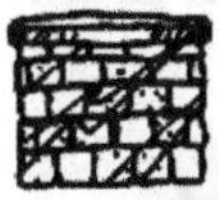 of 1 time each day for 6 days. On day 7, God's  walked 7 times around the 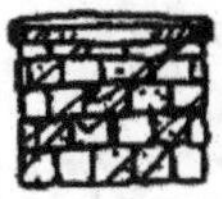 , and when  told the  to shout, the 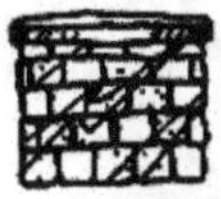 of  fell! All the  of  were killed except  and her family.

Because  had kept God's laws in his  and obeyed Him,  and the  were blessed. And because God always keeps His promises, His chosen  would at last  the promised land!

# Faithful Fighter

Joshua was a soldier of the Lord, fighting for God's chosen people. Did you know that God has promised to fight for *us*? If we keep His love in our hearts and are faithful to Him, God will protect us and fight to keep evil from hurting us.

In the puzzle below, a Scripture verse has been divided into parts. See if you can find each part in the row of letters beside it.

| | | | | | | | | | | |
|---|---|---|---|---|---|---|---|---|---|---|
| | **H** | M | S | L | D | G | E | A | D | F |
| "...the Lord | R | T | H | T | H | E | L | **O** | R | D |
| your God | Y | O | **U** | R | G | O | D | Y | O | R |
| fights | S | F | I | F | I | G | H | T | S | N |
| for you, | T | F | O | R | Y | O | U | F | R | A |
| just | E | T | **J** | U | M | S | J | U | **S** | T |
| as he | O | S | **A** | S | H | E | M | N | O | S |
| promised." | M | R | P | R | O | M | I | S | E | D |
| –Joshua 23:10, NIV | L | T | M | R | P | S | T | L | N | F |

**Try to say this verse by heart!**

Now, unscramble the circled letters in the puzzle above to spell the name of God's warrior.

___ ___ ___ ___ ___ ___ was God's warrior.

**"The Lord is with me. I will not be afraid."**

**—Psalm 118:6**

God has promised to *always* be with you! Each and every day that the sun rises and sets, God will be there—loving you, protecting you, teaching you. Make the Sunrise/Sunset Stick below to help you memorize His promise to you.

**You need:**

one craft stick
two cotton balls

**Directions:**

1. Cut out the patterns and color the suns.

2. Glue the craft stick between the two patterns.

3. Stretch the cotton balls into cloud shapes and glue them on the clouds.

4. Cut out the Scripture strips and glue them on the craft stick (one on the front and one on the back).

"The Lord is with me;
I will not be afraid."

Psalm 118:6

The number **7** stands for perfection and completeness—just as the Lord is perfect and complete! To the people of Israel, **7** was a holy number, for they knew it was a special number to God. The number **7** is found over 379 times in the Bible; more than any other number by far!

In the book of Joshua, the number **7** appears 17 times! God knew His people would see His holy power when He used the number **7** in His commands to Joshua. The power came not from the number **7**, but from the Lord Himself!

See how many times you can find the word **seven** in the puzzle.

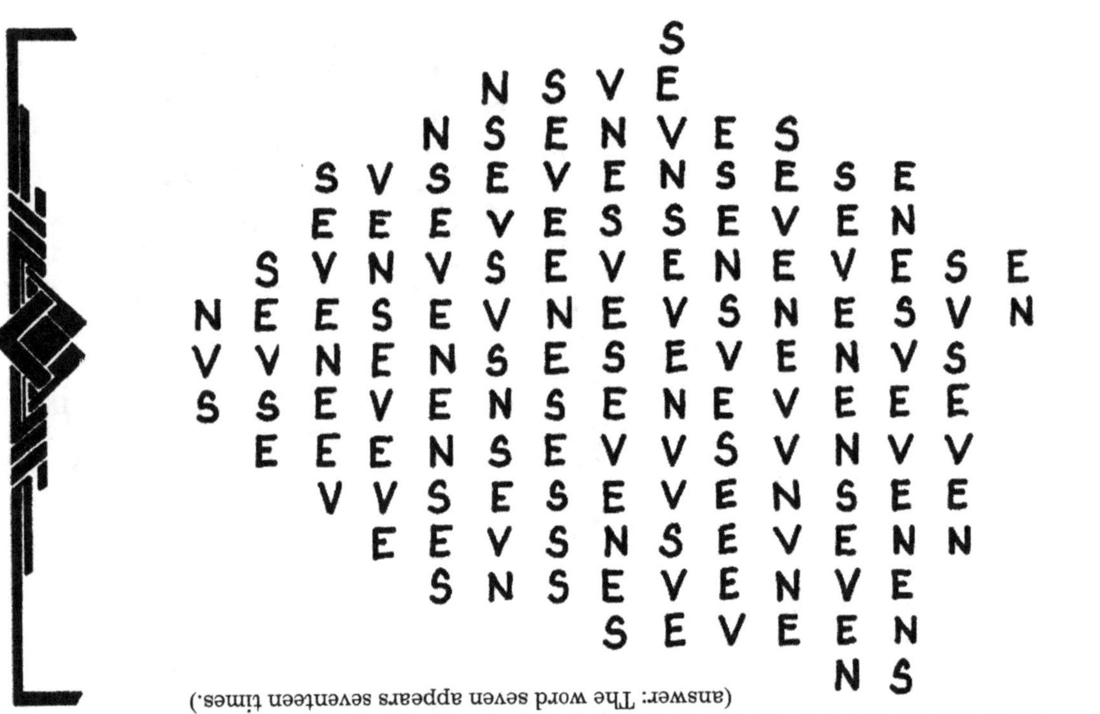


Remember how God lead Joshua to tumble down the wall of Jericho? (Watch those heavenly 7's!)

| | |
|---|---|
| **7** | priests marched in front of the ark of the covenant blowing |
| **7** | trumpets made of rams' horns. On the |
| **7th** | day, the people marched around Jericho |
| **7** | times. After the |
| **7th** | round, Joshua cried to the people: "Shout! For the Lord has given you the city!" Joshua 6:16, NIV<br>And the walls of Jericho fell! |

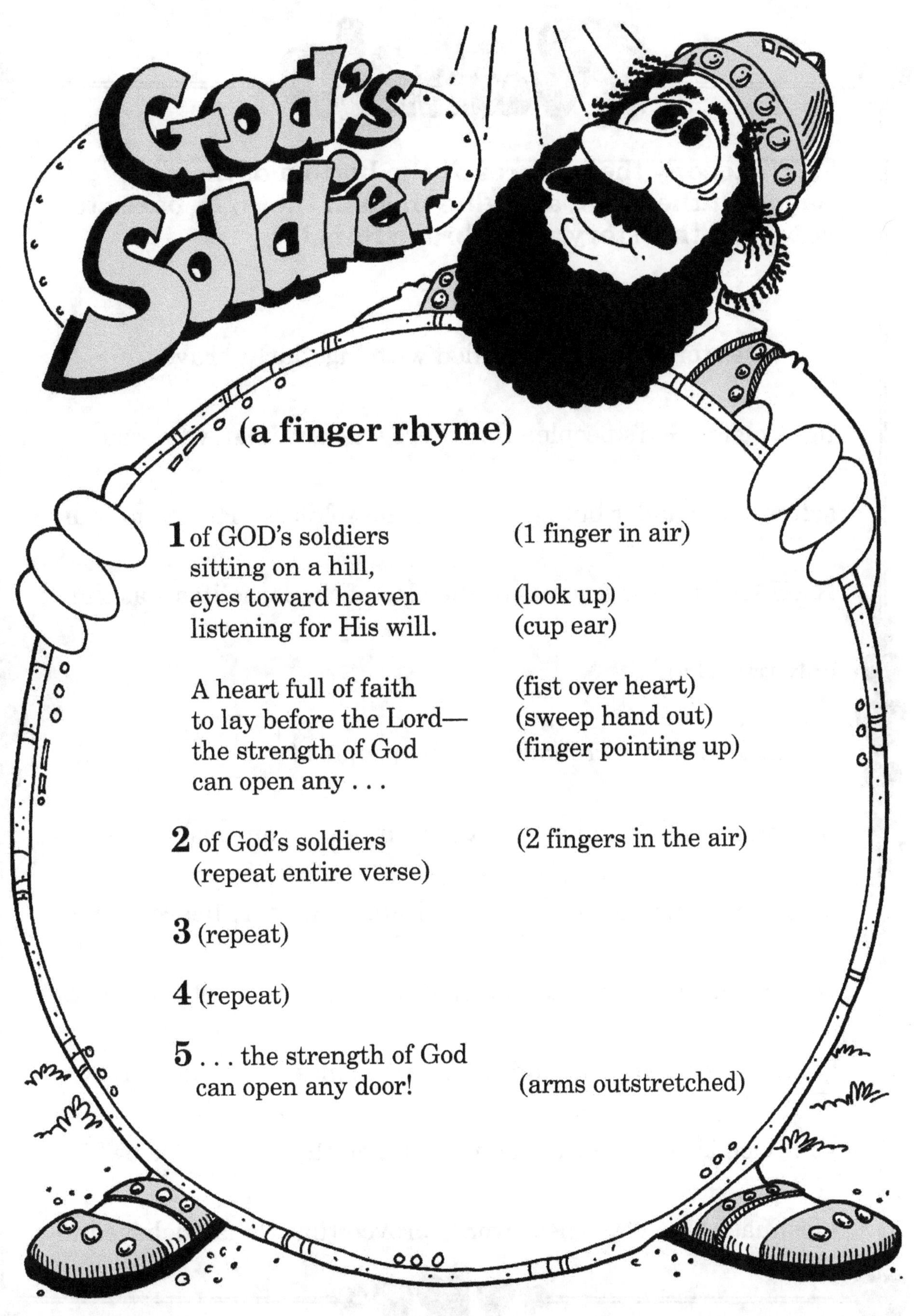


# God's Soldier

(a finger rhyme)

| | |
|---|---|
| **1** of GOD's soldiers | (1 finger in air) |
| sitting on a hill, | |
| eyes toward heaven | (look up) |
| listening for His will. | (cup ear) |
| A heart full of faith | (fist over heart) |
| to lay before the Lord— | (sweep hand out) |
| the strength of God | (finger pointing up) |
| can open any . . . | |
| **2** of God's soldiers | (2 fingers in the air) |
| (repeat entire verse) | |
| **3** (repeat) | |
| **4** (repeat) | |
| **5** . . . the strength of God | |
| can open any door! | (arms outstretched) |

# Rahab

**Photocopy the pictures at the bottom of the next page, cut them out, and glue them in the right boxes to complete this story about brave Rahab.**

The story of Joshua is filled with big, burly, brave [ ] fighting for God's people. But there was a woman who was softer and smaller but as brave as the soldiers! Her name was **RAHAB,** and she knew that the God of the Israelites was the only true God.

Rahab was surrounded by the people of [ ] who did not love God, but Rahab had the courage to help Joshua's spies when they came to her [ ]. Rahab had only heard of the wonderful works of God—she had not seen them with her own [ ]. And yet she said to Joshua's spies " . . . . the Lord your God is God in heaven above and on the [ ] below" (Joshua 2:11, NIV). These words proved that Rahab believed in

the Lord God. The true meaning of faith is believing what you cannot see. Rahab teaches us a wonderful lesson of faith!

Rahab followed the directions of the spies and tied a red cord to her [ ] so that she would be protected by Joshua's soldiers—just as we are under God's protection when we follow His directions. Red is the color that represents courage, and Rahab's [ ] was courageous. The cord was the color of blood—the blood that God would pour out for His [ ].

Rahab is truly a hero in the story of Joshua. And God richly rewarded her for her brave deeds.

# Rahab's Cord

Rahab showed great courage when she decided to hide the spies sent by Joshua. She protected them from the soldiers of her own country because she believed that their God was the one, true God, and she was sure that He would give the Israelites victory over the people of Jericho. She was right; the God of Joshua is *the Lord God of all!* Make a scarlet cord like Rahab's to hang on your door or wall. Each time you look at it, thank God that He is God of all.

**You need:**

- two yards of thick red yarn or cord
- red construction paper
- paper punch
- scissors

**Directions:**

1. Cut three pieces of yarn, each 24" long. Tie them together at one end.
2. Braid the yarn 3/4 of the way down and tie it off. Comb the loose ends to fluff them out.
3. Cut out three red hearts (using the pattern below) and punch a hole in the top of each one.
4. Tie the hearts to the top of the braid with yarn.
5. Cut out the Scripture verse below and punch a hole in the top. Tie to the bottom of the braid.

Who would ever think of fighting an enemy—an entire army!—without one sword, without any weapon at all? Joshua and the people of Israel did–they brought down an entire city surrounded by thick walls without using one weapon. God's battle plan depended on the faith and obedience of His people–and *He* supplied the power!

Like Joshua, we are soldiers in God's army. One of our mightiest weapons against the enemies of God is the shield of faith. Read Epesians 6:10-18 and you will find out how to wear God's armor and be a soldier without a sword (one made of metal, anyway!).

On this puzzle page, words are missing from the list of the armor of God. Use the letter bank below to fill in each missing word. (Hint: Cross out letters as you use them.) The answers may be found in the Ephesians passage given above.

1. Buckle the belt of ______________________.
2. Wear the breastplate of ______________________.
3. Fit your feet with the gospel of ______________________.
4. Take up the shield of ______________________.
5. Put on the helmet of ______________________.
6. Hold the sword of the ______________________.

**"Therefore put on the full armor of God, so that when the day of evil comes, you may be able to stand your ground . . ." Ephesians 6:13,** NIV

Tumble Down
Jericho
Brick Yard

## Use these game pieces to play **Tumble Down Jericho.**

**Preparation:**

1. Cut out the round number card and glue it to cardboard.
2. Cut out the arrow, glue it to thin cardboard, and fasten it to the number card with a brad.
3. Color and cut out the bricks.
4. If you want to make the game pieces last even longer, color everything with marking pens and cover with clear plastic adhesive before cutting things out. (Adhesive won't stick well to crayon.) The game board may be colored and covered, too.

**Directions:**

1. Place the cut-out bricks on the wall of Jericho. Put the extra bricks in the brick yard.
2. Take turns spinning the spinner. If you spin a seven, you may take seven bricks from the wall and place them in the brick yard. If you spin any other number, you must put that many bricks back on the wall. (If the wall is full, add them to the top.)
3. The person to tumble the last brick from the wall is the winner!

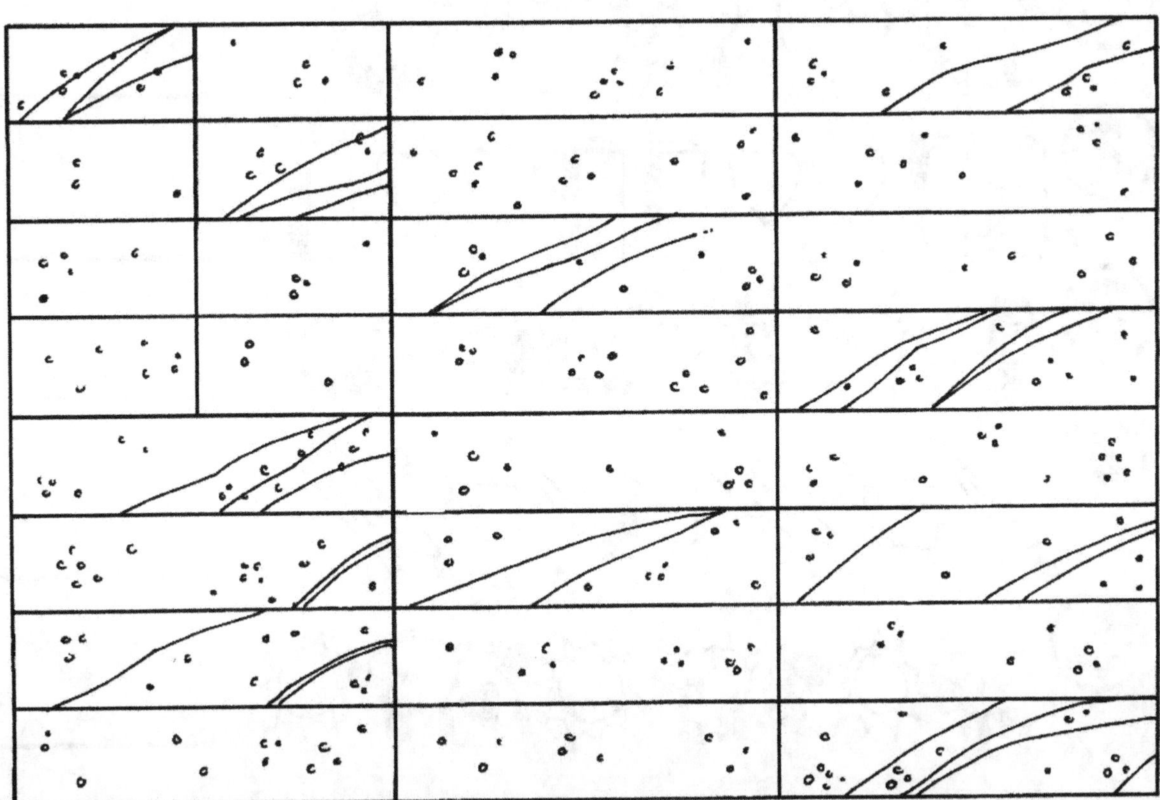

Think back to the last time you played "Simon Says" or "Follow the Leader." When it was time to choose the leader, did you jump up and down and wave your hands in the air crying, "Me! Me! I want to be the leader!"? There is something wonderful about being chosen to lead others, to be the one in charge. It lets us feel wanted and extra special . . . even important!

When you need to choose a leader for your game or classroom, how do you know whom to pick? Your best friend? That boy with the nice smile? Remember Noah, Abraham, Moses, and Joshua? They were all leaders that God chose to lead His people. How does God choose leaders? Does He choose the biggest, bravest men? The strongest or richest men? Noah was not young, Abraham was not strong, Moses was not brave to begin with, and Joshua was not rich—yet God called them to be leaders!

When God calls a leader, He wants a follower! He wants someone who will follow the only true leader—**GOD!** God seeks people who will follow His laws and His Word with all of their hearts, all of their souls, and all of their might! Age, size, money, and strength do not matter to the Lord—only a person with a faithful *following* heart will be a leader for Him!

When God calls us to lead, He wants us to follow Him!

**"Whoever serves me must follow me." John 12:26,** NIV

Look at each row of pictures and see if you can decide what picture comes next.

# You Must Choose...

The Bible says that God is a jealous God. This means that God does not want us to love anyone or anything more than we love Him. If there is something in our lives that distracts us from loving Him, God wants us get rid of that thing. He wants us to choose to give Him *all* of ourselves!

In the puzzle below, each box connects with another box that should contain the same letter. For example, look at the "H" near the beginning. Follow the arrow down to the empty box in the fourth line and place an "H" in that box. Use this method to complete the verse, then check Joshua 24:15, NIV to see if you are correct.

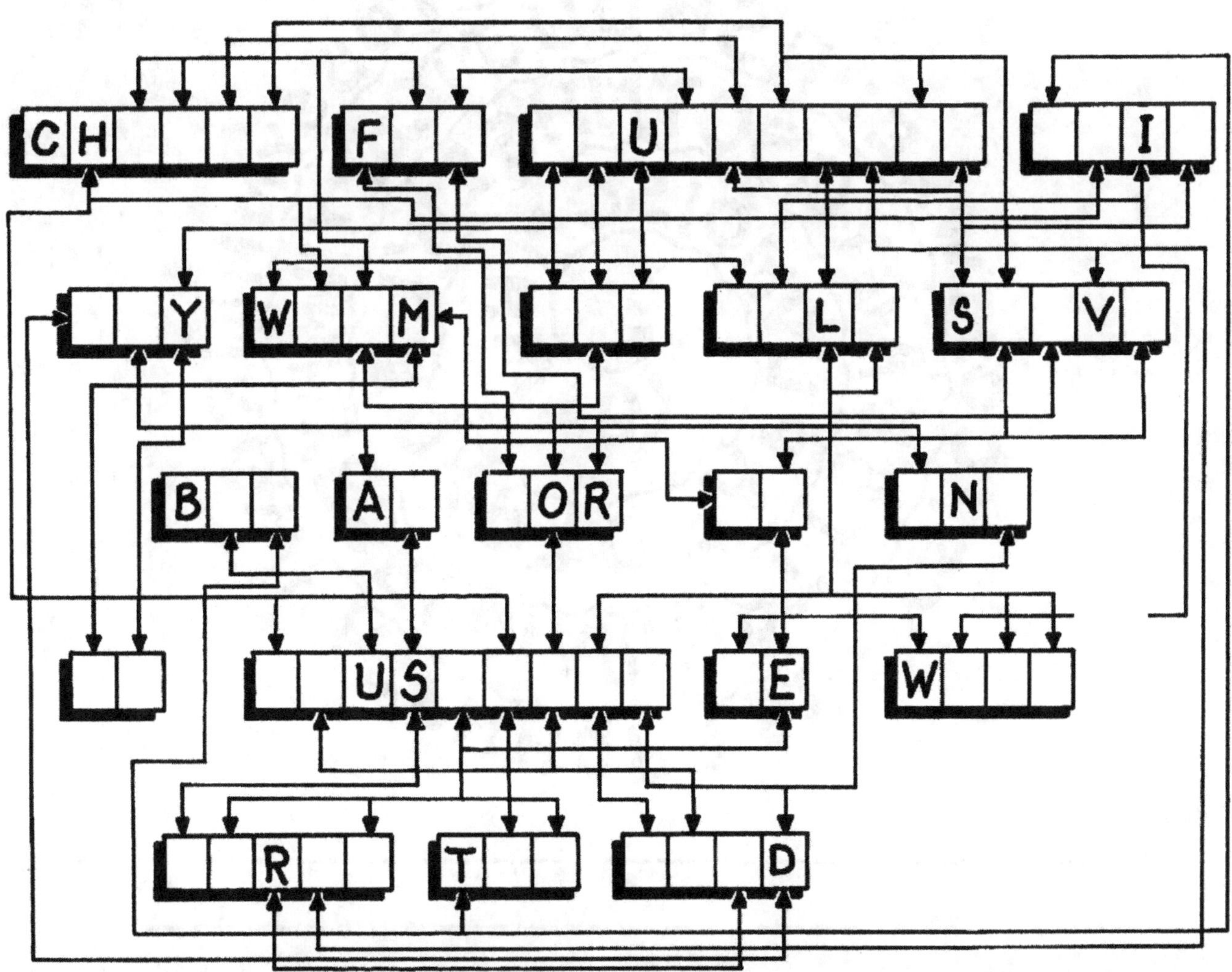


*Joshua 24:15 (NIV)*

Each day, we battle our own "Jerichos." We fight the temptation to do things that God tells us are wrong. We battle bad feelings about the people God wants us to love (like brothers and sisters)! How much we can learn about fighting with faith from the story of Joshua? With faith and total obedience to God, Joshua was able to tumble down the walls of Jericho!

**"By faith the walls of Jericho fell . . . ."** Hebrews 11:30, NIV

Beginning at the star, move around the puzzle and write every other letter in the blank spaces below to spell out how God wants *us* to battle!

"N___ __ ______ ___, __ ______, ___ __ __ _______; ____ ___ ____ _________." Zechariah 4:6, NIV

# Loyal Joshua

Use your NIV Bible to look up **Joshua 24:15** and fill in the missing words to this powerful memory verse and discover what Joshua chose to do. Then color the picture as you think about your own decision to follow and serve God!

"Choose for ________ this day whom you will ________. But as for me and my ________, we will serve the Lord."

—Joshua 24:15

**Open any window; open any door.**
**God has given us glorious gifts**
**to seek, to find, to explore!**

God's gift to Joshua was the strength that comes form faith, obedience, and serving God. Draw a picture of a gift God has given you.

# WISE KING DAVID

**"Teach us to number our days aright, that we may gain a heart of wisdom."**
(Psalm 90:12)

David

King Saul 

Jonathan 

Goliath 

Once there was a king in Israel named . He *had* loved God in his but came proud and began to disobey God. God called His special messenger, Samuel, and told him go to Bethlehem to find a man named Jesse. Jesse had sons, and God would choose of these sons to come king.

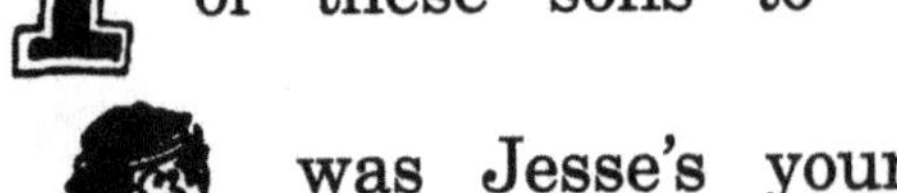 was Jesse's youngest son.  was still a boy—a shepherd who cared  his father's . Samuel told  that God had promised he would be king!

God's were fighting a group of enemies called the Philistines. The Philistines had a  soldier whose name was . was  tall and very ! When  told 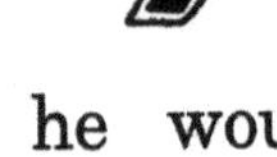 he would fight , looked at 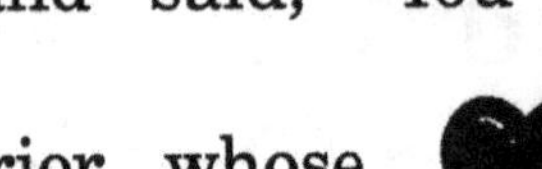 and said, "You are still a boy!" But God a mighty warrior whose was filled with love and faith.

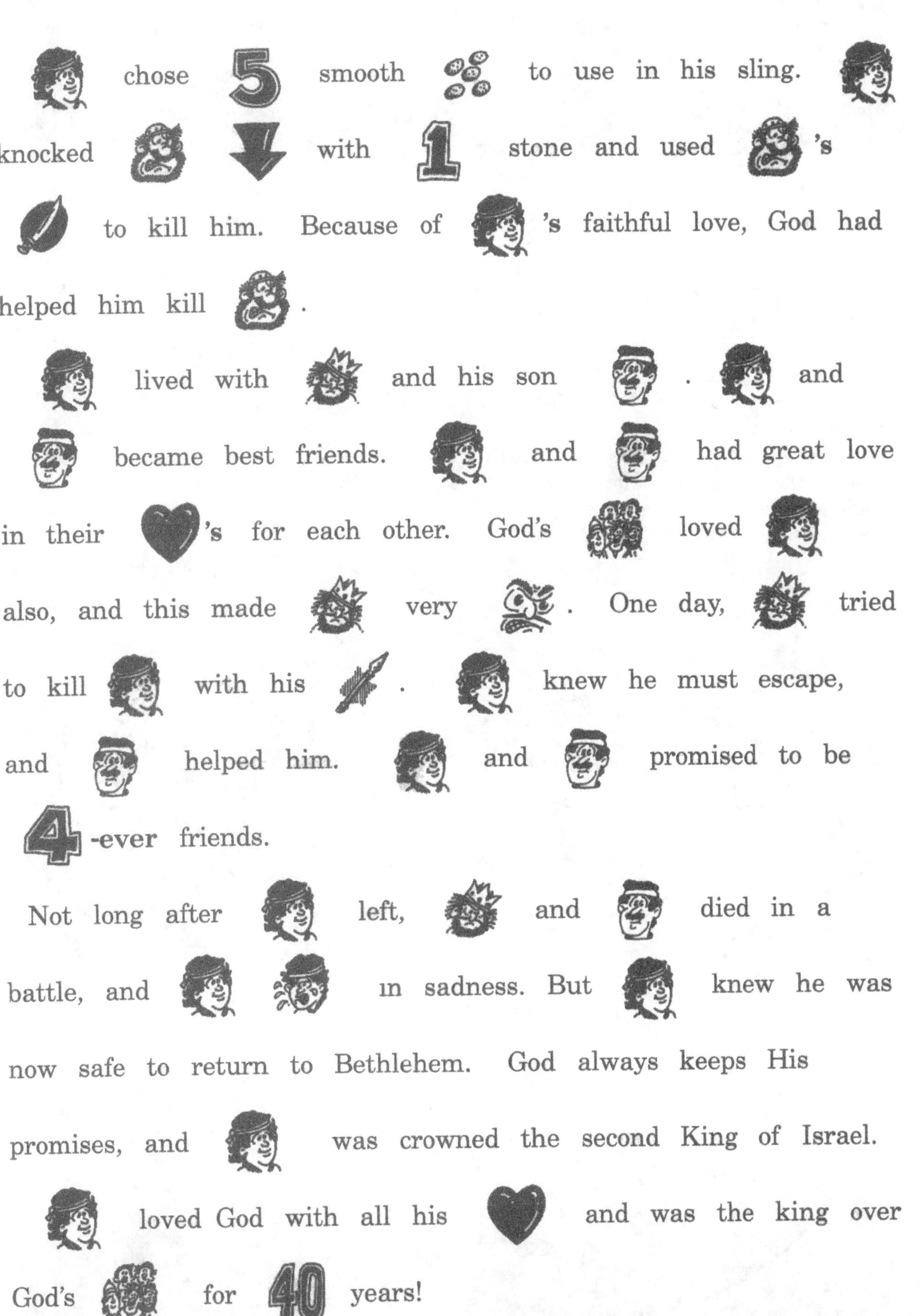

chose 5 smooth to use in his sling. knocked with 1 stone and used 's to kill him. Because of 's faithful love, God had helped him kill .

lived with and his son . and became best friends. and had great love in their 's for each other. God's loved also, and this made very . One day, tried to kill with his . knew he must escape, and helped him. and promised to be 4-ever friends.

Not long after left, and died in a battle, and in sadness. But knew he was now safe to return to Bethlehem. God always keeps His promises, and was crowned the second King of Israel. loved God with all his and was the king over God's for 40 years!

## A game for two or more players.

**To play the game, you need:**
the finished spinner, paper, and pencils, crayons, or markers

**Directions:**

1. Cut out arrow and circle below. Glue both to tagboard and attach arrow to circle with a paper fastener.
2. Player one spins and draws on paper the part of the sheep that is spun. The spinner must land on the head before each player can draw the ears, eyes, or nose and on the body before drawing legs or tail.
3. The first player to complete his or her sheep is the winner!

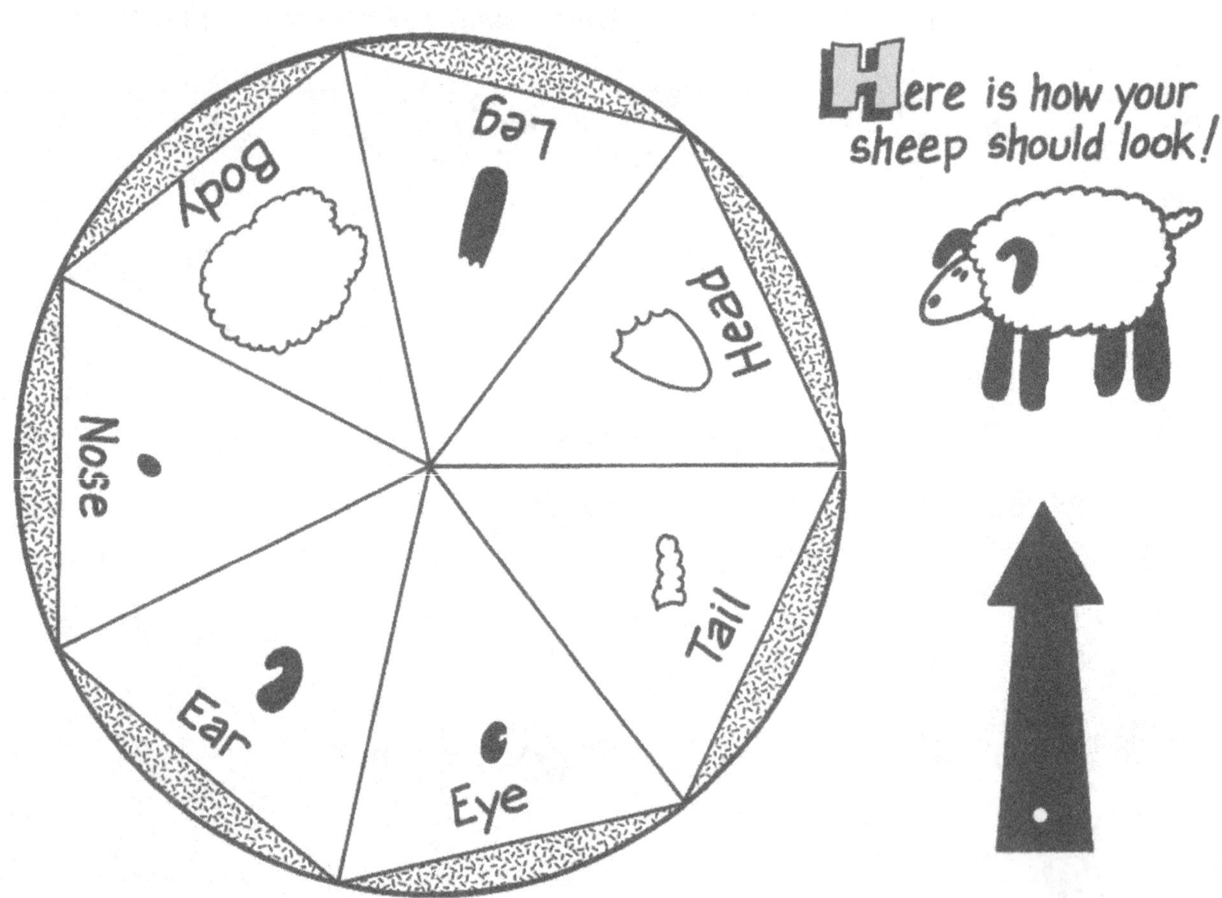

# Little Ones (PUPPET) Lamb

**You need:**

two paper fasteners
two craft sticks
paper punch
cotton balls
scissors
glue

**Directions:**

1. Cut out lamb and his two legs.
2. Attach them to tagboard to make them more sturdy.
3. Glue cotton balls onto lamb to make him fluffy.
4. Using paper punch, punch holes at the top of the legs and bottom of the body. Attach legs to body using the paper fasteners.
5. Glue (or staple) craft sticks to back of legs. (Let dry!)

Now let your lamb "dance" and "leap" with joy by moving the sticks!

Finish the story below by cutting out the pictures at the bottom of this page and gluing them in any blank box you choose! Won't the story sound a tiny bit strange? You bet! And you'll have some GIANT laughs as you read it!

In a land far, far away, lived a fierce **GIANT!** He had a nose as big as a [ ], hair that he brushed with a [ ] and he wore a green [ ] around his waist. All of the people in the land were very much afraid of *the GIANT. He ate the* [ ] **'s** that belonged to the people, and he used their [ ] **'s** for his toys! Whenever the townspeople saw the GIANT, they would hide in their [ ] **'s**—for his temper was frightful, and he treated the people like itty-bitty bugs beneath his feet!

One day, a tiny stranger came to the land. He was smaller than a [ ] and wore odd-looking glasses that slipped down his nose. When asked why he wore such strange glasses, the wee stranger pushed them up on his nose and replied, "They help my heart to see better!" *See... with his heart!?* wondered the townspeople. But before they could ask any questions, someone began to shout, **"LOOK! LOOK!"** The GIANT was tromping toward them with a [ ] in his fist and a mean smile curling his lip!

The tiny stranger squinted through his odd glasses at the townspeople and calmly asked, "Why are you so afraid?"

"Are you *blind?*" they cried. "He is *so big!*"

The tiny stranger peered more closely at the GIANT and replied, "No, I am not blind, but perhaps *you* are. Why are you afraid of one so small?"

Upon hearing this, the giant stopped. **"Small?!"** he bellowed! **"But I am a GIANT!"**

"Sir, you are mistaken," said the stranger. "You are really quite small indeed! Why, you are tinier than the tiniest [ ] !"

The giant looked at his feet— he could not believe what he had heard!

"Yes, small indeed," repeated the wee one. "Your small behavior shows me that you think very little of yourself." The GIANT, suddenly feeling very small and very afraid of this tiny man, burst into a run, headed straight for his [ ] to hide, and was never seen again!

"How . . . how . . ." stammered the townspeople.

"You see," explained the tiny stranger, wiping his odd glasses on his sleeve, "you have been seeing the GIANT only with your eyes, and so you noticed only his size. I saw the GIANT with my heart and could see how truly tiny he was inside! His actions were tiny, his courage was tiny, but tiniest of all was his heart. God wants us to see with our hearts as well as our eyes, and then we will be able to see better. You were blind to how truly tiny the GIANT is!"

In an instant, the townspeople learned of God's gift of a seeing heart, and they knew they had seen a tiny GIANT conquered by a GIANT tiny!

**Word Bank**
LARGE
MONSTROUS
HULKING
JUMBO
GIGANTIC
MOUNTAINOUS
HUGE
MASSIVE
BIG
GIANT
HUMONGUS
GOLIATH

vmintbitsynm
esmallbhlvhi
rohmenietmkn
tinyiotyoeti
smelnteensya
lnos
init
thne
tamv
lmia
eind
hnii
meag
istu
nluv
umre
taeb
esgd
kwee

iny
Word Hunt

**Word Bank**
MINUTE
SMALL
TEENSY
MINI
LITTLE
BITSY
WEE
MINIATURE
TINY

# In The Eyes of the Beholder

When King Saul looked at David, he said, "You are not able to go out against this Philistine and fight him; you are only a boy, and he has been a fighting man from his youth" (1 Samuel 17:33, NIV). He saw David as a youth, small and inexperienced. How could he win a fight with a *giant*?

Yet when God, the Beholder, saw David, He saw a brave warrior! He saw beyond skin and muscle, straight into David's heart, which was filled with faith and love!

When we look at David the shepherd, perhaps we only see a boy leading sheep to greener grass and water, a boy who was not rich and did not have a famous family. But when the Beholder saw David the shepherd, He saw the heart of a mighty king! He saw a heart that loved all the human "sheep" he would one day lead!

Our human eyes see only what is on the outside. But the true Beholder, God, looks inside our hearts. and minds. He sees what kind of people we really are, and because He is God, He loves us anyway.

"The Lord does not look at the things man looks at. Man looks at the outward appearance, but the Lord looks at the heart." 1 Samuel 16:7, NIV

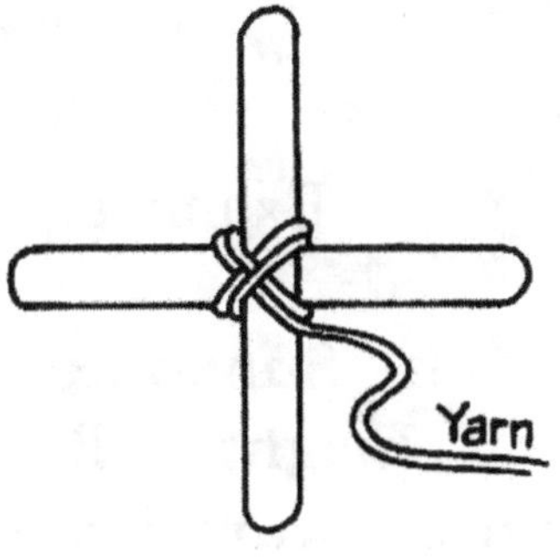


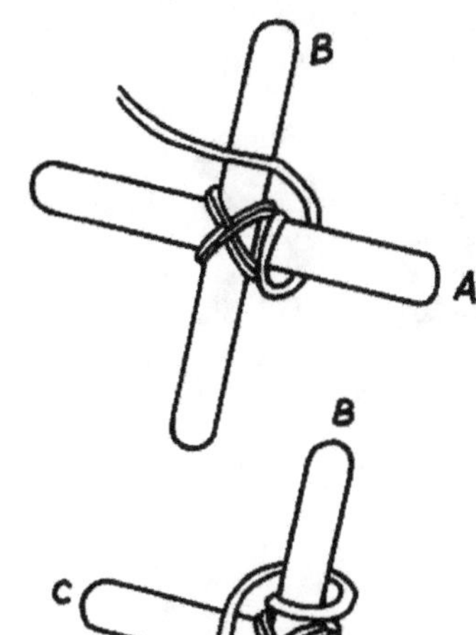


**You need:**

ball of yarn (Multi-colored yarn works nicely.)
two craft sticks

**Directions:**

1. Hold sticks in the shape of a cross and wrap yarn crisscross a few times over the center to hold the sticks and the end of the yarn in place.
2. Then wrap the yarn once around stick A, then cross to stick B.
3. Wrap yarn around stick B and cross to stick C. Now wrap and cross to D.
4. Continue in a round and round pattern until you have covered all but 1/2" of each stick. Then bring yarn to backside, loop end under yarn and tie off.

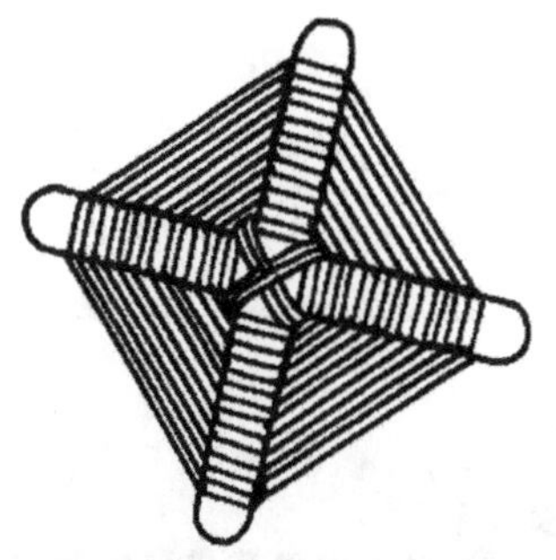

"God's Eyes" make beautiful ornaments to hang in your window or on a Christmas tree!

# David's Talents

David was a man of many talents. Some believe that he was the most talented of all the people in the Bible. What were his talents?

In addition to being a good shepherd and a great warrior king, David was a musician and a poet. He played the lute and the harp. Remember that Saul's servants sent for David when they wanted the best harpist for Saul. As a poet, David wrote many of the psalms (songs) found in our Bible. Is it hard to be a poet? No. You can write poems too!

You can write a special kind of poem by following this pattern and directions.

Title (noun)
2 describing words
3 action words
4 words that describe feelings about the subject
1 synonym for (a word that means the same thing as) the title

Example:

**Sunshine**
**bright, yellow**
**shining, warming, glowing**
**happy, smiling, wonderful, playful**
**Light**

Now you try!

______________

______________, ______________

______________, ______________, ______________

______________, ______________, ______________, ______________

______________

# My Best Friend

Who is like a friend to me?
Who cares through thick and thin?
Who always thinks I'm beautiful,
Whatever shape I'm in?
Who's the one who always seems
To know my heartfelt thoughts and dreams?
Who is this gift from God?
**MY BEST FRIEND!**
And I will love you 'till the end!

David and Jonathan loved each other very much. They spent lots of time together. They gave each other gifts. They helped each other. Jonathan even saved David's life! David and Jonathan were wonderful God-gifts to each another; they were best friends!

Read the following Scripture verse, then see if you can fit each word into the puzzle.

**"But there is a friend who sticks closer than a brother."**
(Proverbs 18:24, NIV)

**Who is the Friend who sticks closer than a brother?** ____________

# Give your FRIEND a lift!

Color the mini-poster below. Cut on the dotted line, and give your poster to a friend. You'll both get a real lift (and a smile)!

# Looking At David's Heart

God called David "**. . . a man after my own heart.**" (Acts 13:22, NIV)

If David was a man after God's own heart, then perhaps if we take a look at David's heart, we will have a tiny glimmer of the beauty in God's heart.

Make David's heart whole by cutting out the puzzle pieces below and gluing them on a sheet of construction paper. Then read about the heart of one who loved God with his *whole* heart!

# Fruits of the Heart

Look up the Scripture verse in each of the grapes. (You will need an NIV Bible to do this page.) If the verse and the reference match, color the grape. If they do not match, leave the grape white.

What shape have you colored?

Now write the underlined words in the grapes on the lines below. You will have a list of fruits that God wants us to grow in our hearts!

________________ ________________ ________________

________________ ________________ ________________

________________ ________________ ________________

________________ ________________ ________________

# When He Looks

*Read the poem and then do the activity on the next page as a reminder that God doesn't look at the outside of a person; He looks at his or her heart!*

I've often wondered,
  When God looks at me
As He peers down from Heaven,
  Just what does He see?

Does He notice my hair?
  Should I dress more like you?
Does He care if my clothing
  Is worn or is new?

Does He like me only
  Because of my eyes?
Too tall or too big—
  Does He notice my size?

Can He see the big trophy
  I won on that hike?
Does He notice how great
  I am on my bike?

Does He look at my school work
  And if I can add?
If He doesn't see A's,
  Will He think I am bad?

I know that as humans
  When we look at others,
We see only the outside
  Of our friends and our brothers.

But God looks deeper;
  He spreads me apart.
When God looks at me,
  He looks into my heart!

# Spread-Apart Heart

**Make a heart to spread apart to remind you of how God sees!**

**You need:**

white and red construction paper
a small photograph of yourself
crayon or marking pen
a paper fastener

**Directions:**

1. Using the patterns on this page, cut a white heart using the full heart pattern and a red heart using the two half-heart patterns.
2. Glue the photograph of yourself to the center of the white heart.
3. Overlap the two half-heart pieces and connect them to the white heart at the point indicated by the little circle.
4. Carefully holding the pieces so they won't shift, write the words from 1 Samuel 16:7 on the red heart. (If using a marking pen, place a piece of paper under the red heart to absorb any ink bleeding through.)

Now as you read the poem "When He Looks," spread apart your heart to reveal whose heart God sees!

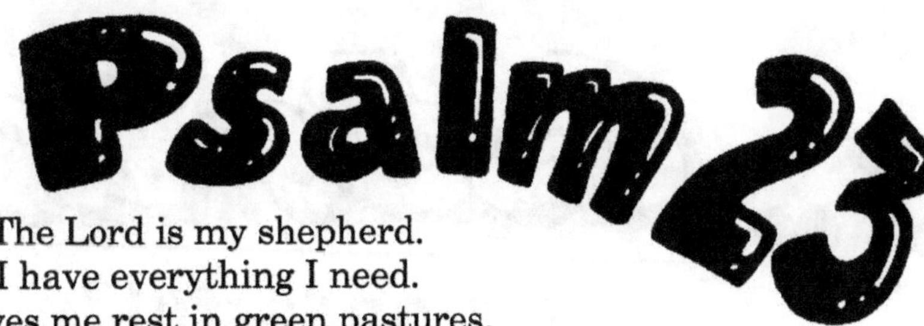


The Lord is my shepherd.
I have everything I need.
He gives me rest in green pastures.
He leads me to calm water.
He gives me new strength.
For the good of his name, he leads me on paths that are right.
Even if I walk through a very dark valley,
I will not be afraid because you are with me.
Your rod and your walking stick comfort me.
You prepare a meal for me in front of my enemies.
You pour oil on my head.
You give me more than I can hold.
Surely your goodness and love will be with me all my life.
And I will live in the house of the Lord forever.

*(ICB)*

David loved to write poems. He wrote about things he did every day. As a shepherd, he would sit in the pastures and by calm waters and think about God's loving care for him.

If you were to write a poem, using David's poem as a model, how would you describe how God cares for you? Can you memorize the 23rd Psalm?

The Lord is my ____________________. I have everything that I need.

He gives me rest in ______________________________.

He leads me to ______________________________.

He gives me ________________________.

For the good of his name, he leads me on paths that are right.

Even if I walk ______________________________,

I will not be afraid because you are with me.

Your ______________ and your ______________ comfort me.

You prepare a ______________ for me in the presence of my enemies.

You ____________________________________________.

You give me more than I can hold.

Surely your ______________ and ______________ will be with me all my life.

And I will live in the house of the Lord forever.

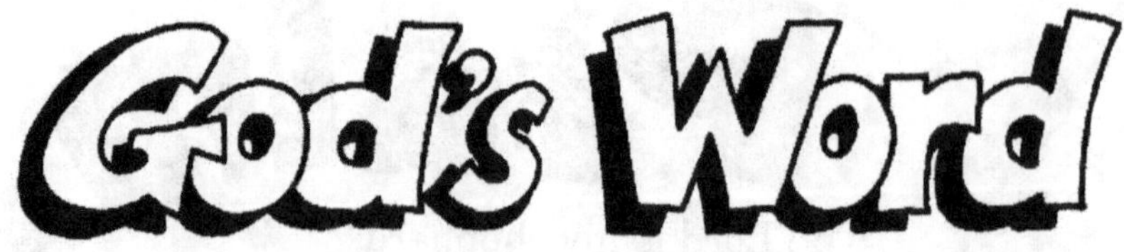

God blesses us in many ways, and we have many reasons to thank Him! Make the "Thank-You, God!" bag shown below, to help you remember this Scripture verse:

**You need:**

white, brown, or pastel-colored lunch bag
things for decorating the bag
(glitter, lace, ribbons, etc.)
markers
glue

**Directions:**

1. Write the Scripture verse above on a slip of paper and glue it to the front of the lunch bag. (Or you may photocopy the Scripture box above, color it, cut it out, and paste it on your bag.) On the back of the bag, print the words: THANK YOU, GOD!

2. Decorate your bag with markers, glitter, etc.

3. Every day for a week, draw a small picture of something you are thankful for and put the picture in your bag. In a week, share your thanksgivings with your class or family.

# Wise King David

Use your NIV Bible to look up **Psalm 90:12** and fill in the missing words to this powerful memory verse to discover what David filled his heart with. Then color the picture as you think about how God and His Word give you wisdom and understanding.

"Teach us to

__________

our days

__________,

that we may

__________

a heart of

__________."

—Psalm 90:12

**Open any window; open any door.**
**God has given us glorious gifts**
**to seek, to find, to explore!**

God's gift to David was the wisdom and power that comes from faith and obedience. Draw a picture of a gift God has given you.

# PRAYERFUL DANIEL

**"Be joyful in hope, patient in affliction, faithful in prayer."** (Romans 12:12)

Daniel  Shadrach, Meshach, Abednego  King Nebuchadnezzar  King Darius 

Once there was a king in the land of Babylon who did not have God in his . His name was . went to the city of Jerusalem with and destroyed it. He captured some of God's and brought them back 2 Babylon to serve him. Among these were 4 young men named and . and had God in their , and although they missed Jerusalem, they were alone 4 God was with them!

worshiped idols and tried to make and 4 get about God by teaching them about Babylon and giving them his and . But and were faithful to God and would not eat the or drink the  from .

had strange dreams in his  at , and God gave the wisdom to tell what the dreams meant. To reward 's wisdom, gave and important jobs in Babylon. 1 day, made an idol of that was 90 tall and ordered all the to bow and worship it instead of God. were faithful to God and said, "NO!" came very and threw into a furnace of . Then and "1 like the of God" walking in the ! God had sent an to save .

remained faithful to God and 3 times every day. When he was about 80 years old, a new king named ordered everyone to pray to him. Faithful would not, so put in a den of s. But God sent an to close the of the s and was not harmed!

Because was faithful 2 God, and because God always keeps His promises to those who are faithful, lived in peace and God gave him a special of being able to see into the years 2 come!

# Fitting Faith

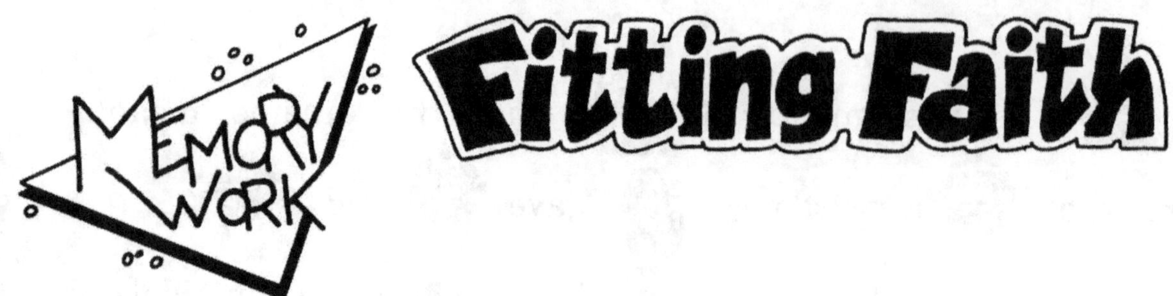

Fit each word of the verse below into the puzzle. Some of the letters are already in place to get you started. Can you memorize this verse as you work on the puzzle?

**They trusted in him and defied the king's command and were willing to give up their lives rather than serve or worship any god except their own God.**

**Daniel 3:28 b, NIV**

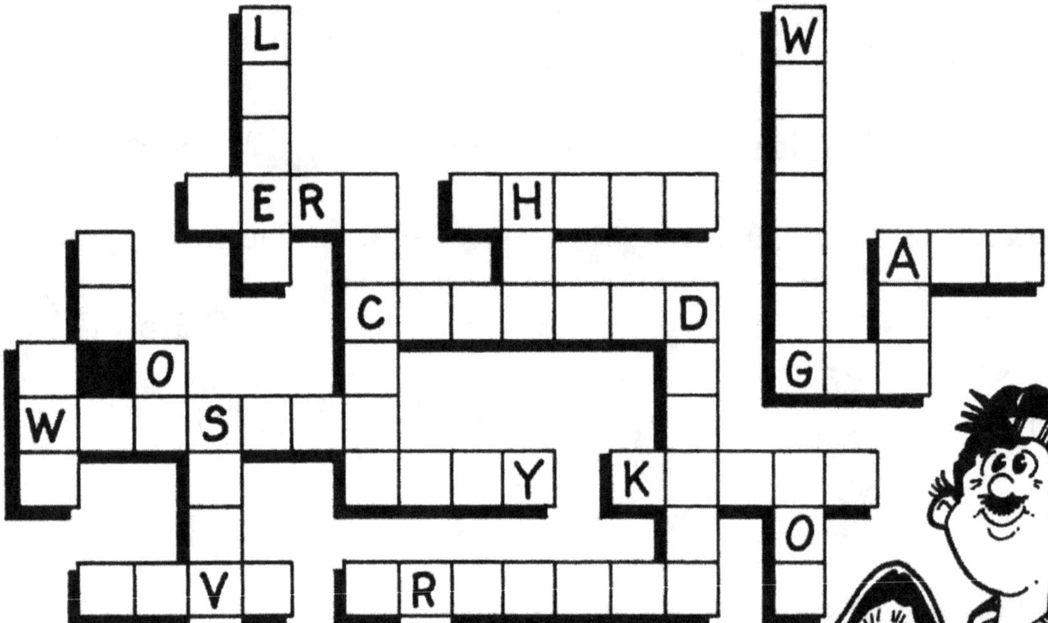

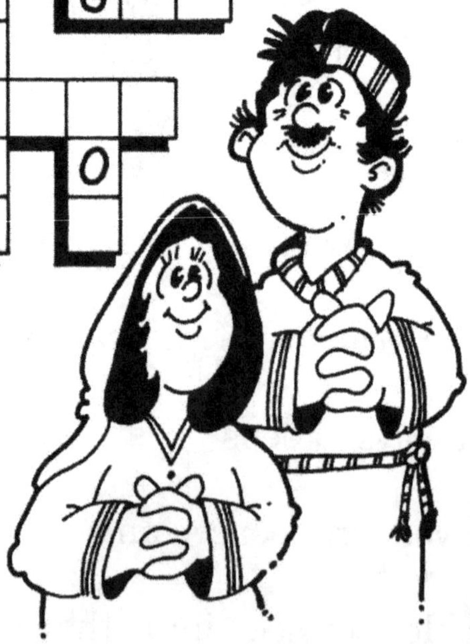

# The Heat Is On

**Find your way out of this maze of flames!**

# Serve Only The Lord

How can a young person live a pure life?
He can do it by obeying your word.
*Psalm 119:9, ICB*

**How did Daniel obey God's Word?**
**Decode the Scripture below for the answer.**

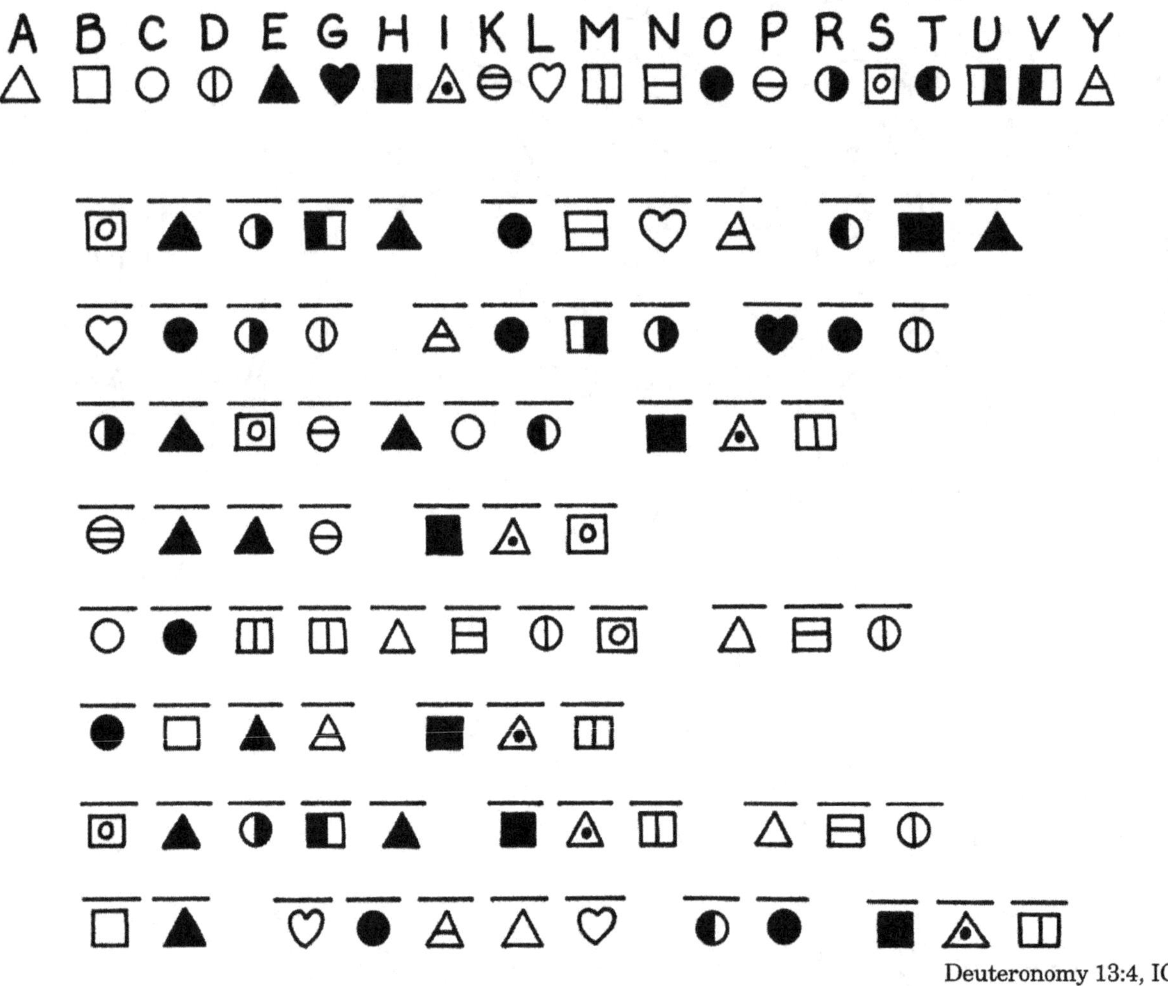


Deuteronomy 13:4, ICB

**Now go back and circle five different things we are to do to live God's Word. (One is so important that it's listed twice!) Hint: Look for verbs.**

# The Hanging Gardens of Babylon

Long ago, people from all over the world would come to Babylon to see Nebuchadnezzar's amazing hanging gardens. These gardens were planted on a man-made mountain called a pyramid. There were five levels or terraces, each planted with beautiful trees, bushes, and flowers.

Inside the terraced-garden pyramid were rooms that stayed cool in the summer because of all the dirt and plants overhead. In these rooms, government officials and businessmen had meetings. In a special room in the center of the pyramid, underground, was a deep well. Over the well a machine was built to draw water to the plants on all the terraces. The machine was very complicated.

Why did Nebuchadnezzar build this incredible pyramid? He built it for his wife who was from a part of the world that had mountains. She missed the mountains of her homeland and the king wanted her to be happy in Babylon, so he ordered the garden built. This wonderful garden is still known as one of the "seven wonders of the world."

## Make Your Own Hanging Garden!

**You need:**

- sphagnum moss (You can buy this at nurseries and florist shops.)
- string, cord
- spray bottle of water
- seeds (peas, beans, radishes, squash, etc.)
- pencil

**Here's How:**

1. Spray a large clump of moss with water.
2. Pat the moss into a large ball (about 4" in diameter) and wind the string around and around it to hold it together. Tie a long piece of strong string or cord to the top for hanging the ball.
3. With the pencil, push seeds into the damp ball. Use plenty of seeds!
4. Lightly spray the ball with water and hang in a sunny window. (Spray lightly every other day.)

In a week or two, you will have a beautiful hanging garden to enjoy!

# Hide His Word in Your Heart

What can you do when you are afraid? God tells us that if we will trust Him, He will take away our fears.

On the blanks below, write the letter that comes after each letter given (below the blank). Then cut out the boxes and put your verse in order by matching the shapes in the corner of the boxes to the shapes in the boxes at the bottom of the page.

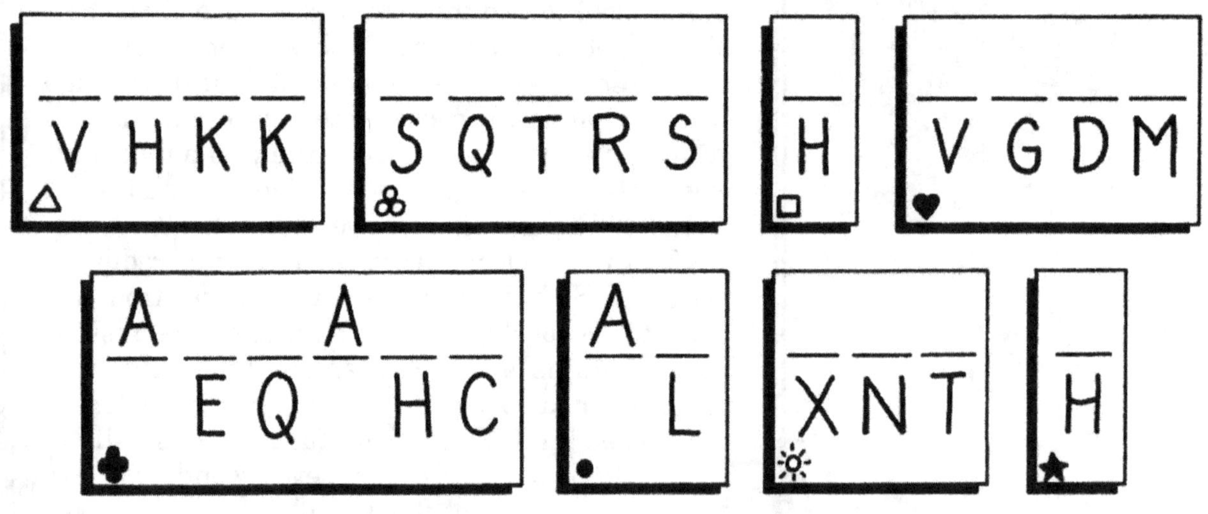


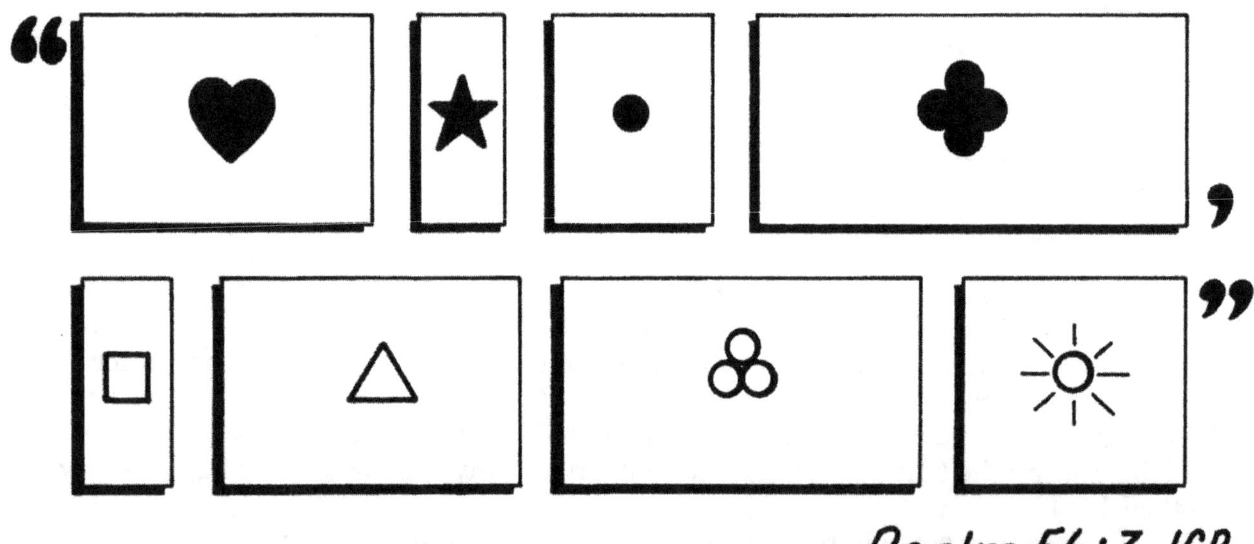

Psalm 56:3, ICB

# Little Angel

*(Sing to the tune of "Mary Had a Little Lamb")*

Little angel next to me

I am safe

because of thee;

For I know you protect me.

Angels all around!

**Write the first letter of each picture in the space above it.
What heavenly word did you spell?**

# Daniel's Mobile

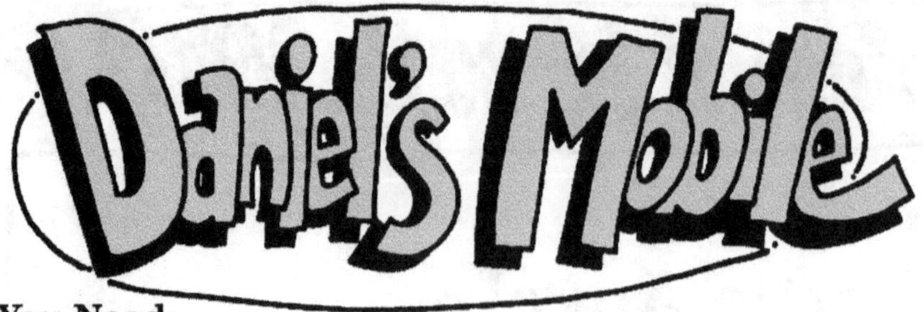

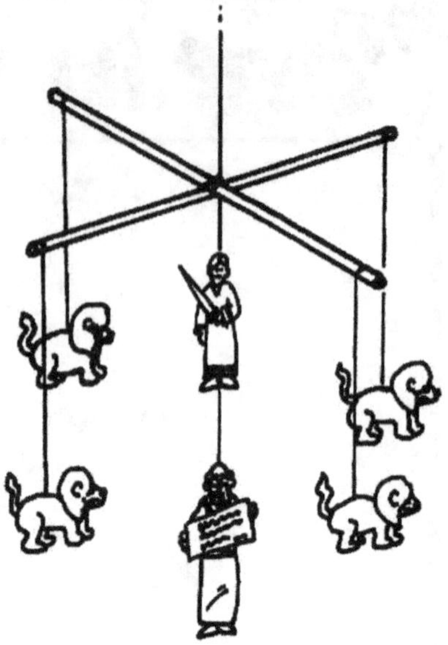

**You Need:**
- 2 straws or 2 thin dowel rods cut to about 12"
- fishing line
- clear tape
- crayons

**Directions:**
1. Holding your straws or rods in the shape of a cross, wrap fishing line around the center to hold them in place.
2. Tie one long piece of line to the middle to hang the mobile.
3. Cut out the figures of Daniel and the angel from this page.
4. Trace the lion figure onto brown construction paper and cut out four.
5. Color the figures.
6. Assemble according to the diagram using tape to hold the shapes to the fishing line.

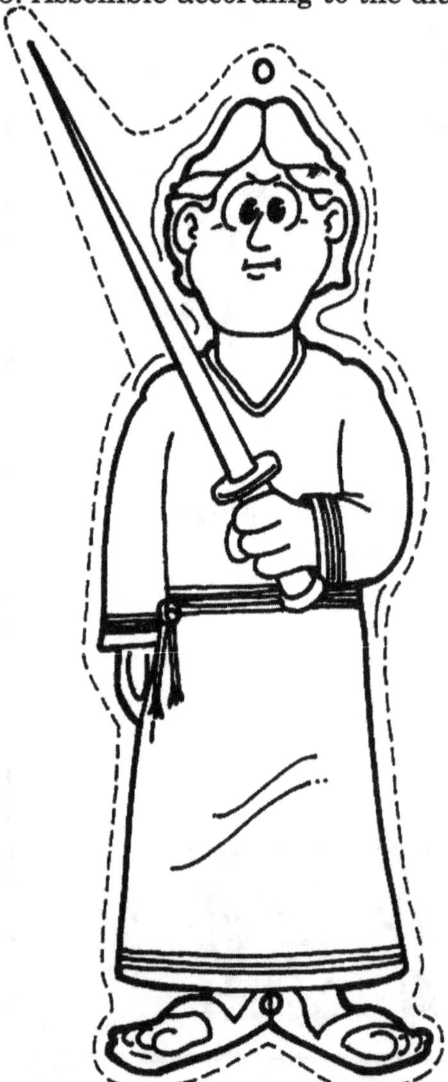

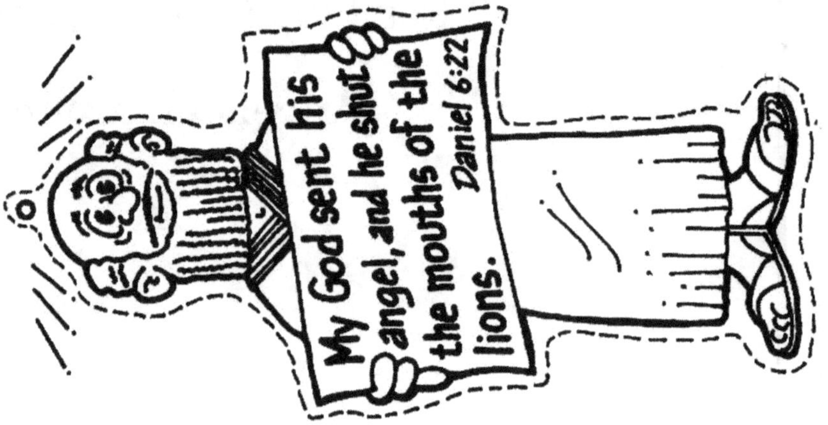

My God sent his angel, and he shut the mouths of the lions.
Daniel 6:22

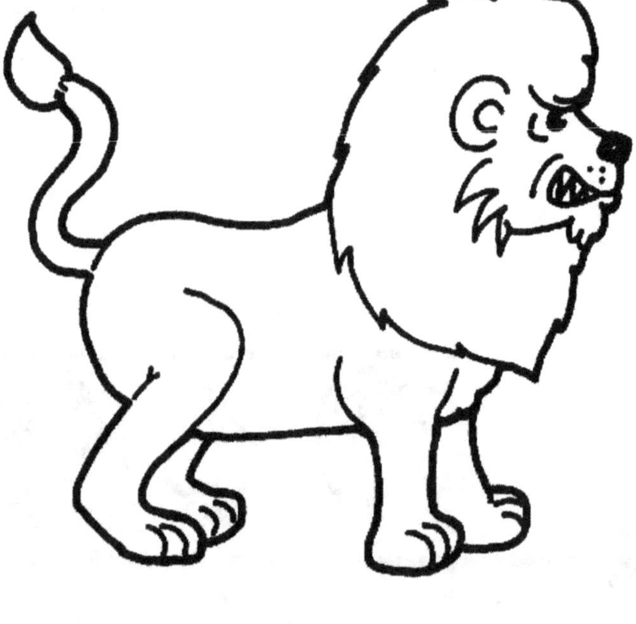

Quincy has been learning about Daniel's faithfulness to God. But he still has questions. Using the code below, help Quincy find the answers to his questions.

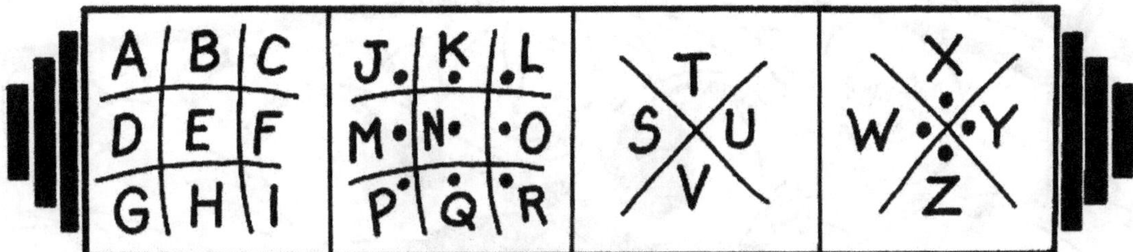


**Q:** Did God tempt Daniel to stop praying?

**A:**

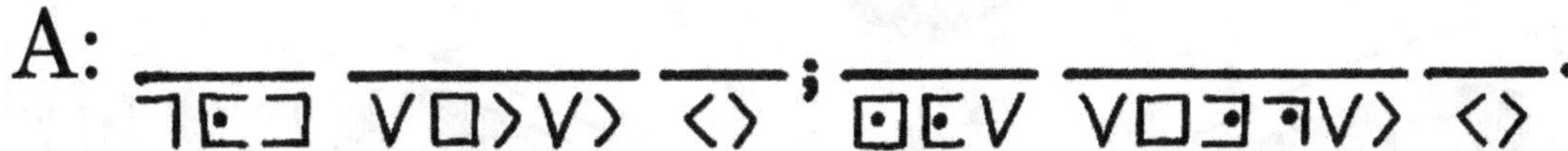

God did not tempt Daniel to stop praying, but He may have used the temptation to test Daniel's faith and obedience. He also used the opportunity to show His power to all the Babylonians!

**Q:** God could have zapped Daniel away from danger—why didn't He?

**A:**

Taking Daniel away from trouble would have been the easy way out. God loved Daniel enough to let him grow by walking through his troubles.

**Q:** Was God punishing Daniel?

**A:**

Daniel's faith was strong, yet God wanted him to become even stronger! Daniel allowed himself to be like a lump of clay to be molded and shaped by the Master Potter! Will you choose to be the same way?

No Lion!
BEWARE! This is a hungry animal! See if you can find the words listed on the sides before he gobbles them up!
N E B U C H A D N E Z Z A R S
O R H R A E B S T O R Y R E B
W S F D B S E R L I O N S P A
I H W S E A D D R A S J W R B
S A Y E D T N P O N R D H A Y
D D P R A Y E R I G A R B G L
O R I L R V G A T E B E S T O
M A N E I H O U F L Y A D E N
F C L P U R Y E A O P M A L M
R H N A S O M U I A R S N H O
F U R N A C E S T D N E I N R
I L E D Y O S C H B A L E P T
E N M I E S H A F I W S L B A
R D F M R T A J U W R E S I L
Y O S H E A C A L E B D E O A
O P A Y R R H N E F B M B S B
Faithful
Dreams
Prayer
Abednego
Daniel
Nebuchadnezzar
Furnace
Den
Fiery
Shadrach
Meshach
Lions
Angel
Babylon
Wisdom
Darius

What are the most important things in your life? Think! Think! Think!

In box 1, draw the *most* important thing in your life. In box 2, draw the next most important thing. Continue for boxes 3, 4, and 5.

Now, pretend you *must* give up what is in box 5. Could you? How about box 4, box 3, box 2? Look at box 1—could you give up **the most important thing in your life?**

Daniel shows us that we must put God in our "first" box. Daniel was ready to give up his life because of his faith in God! The story of Daniel calls us to have a new kind of love for God—love that will never stop, love for which we would give up everything!

(Note: Teacher/parent sensitivity in this discussion is very important!)

**PRECIOUS LOVE**

What would I give up
For Your love?

Can *things* be as precious
As my God above?

I'd give all away
To stay faithful and true,

For nothing's as precious
In my life as You!

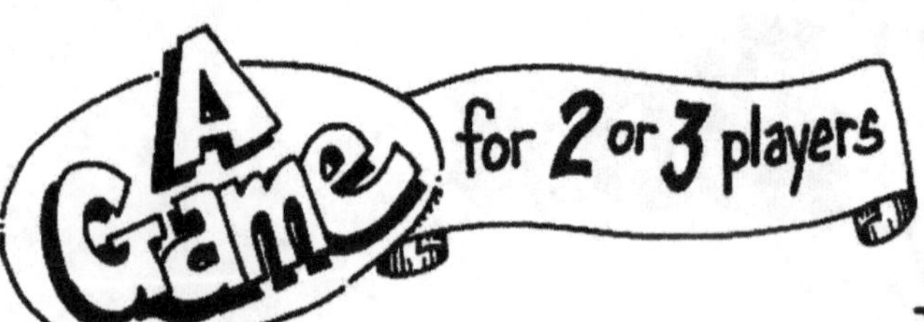

## A Game for 2 or 3 players

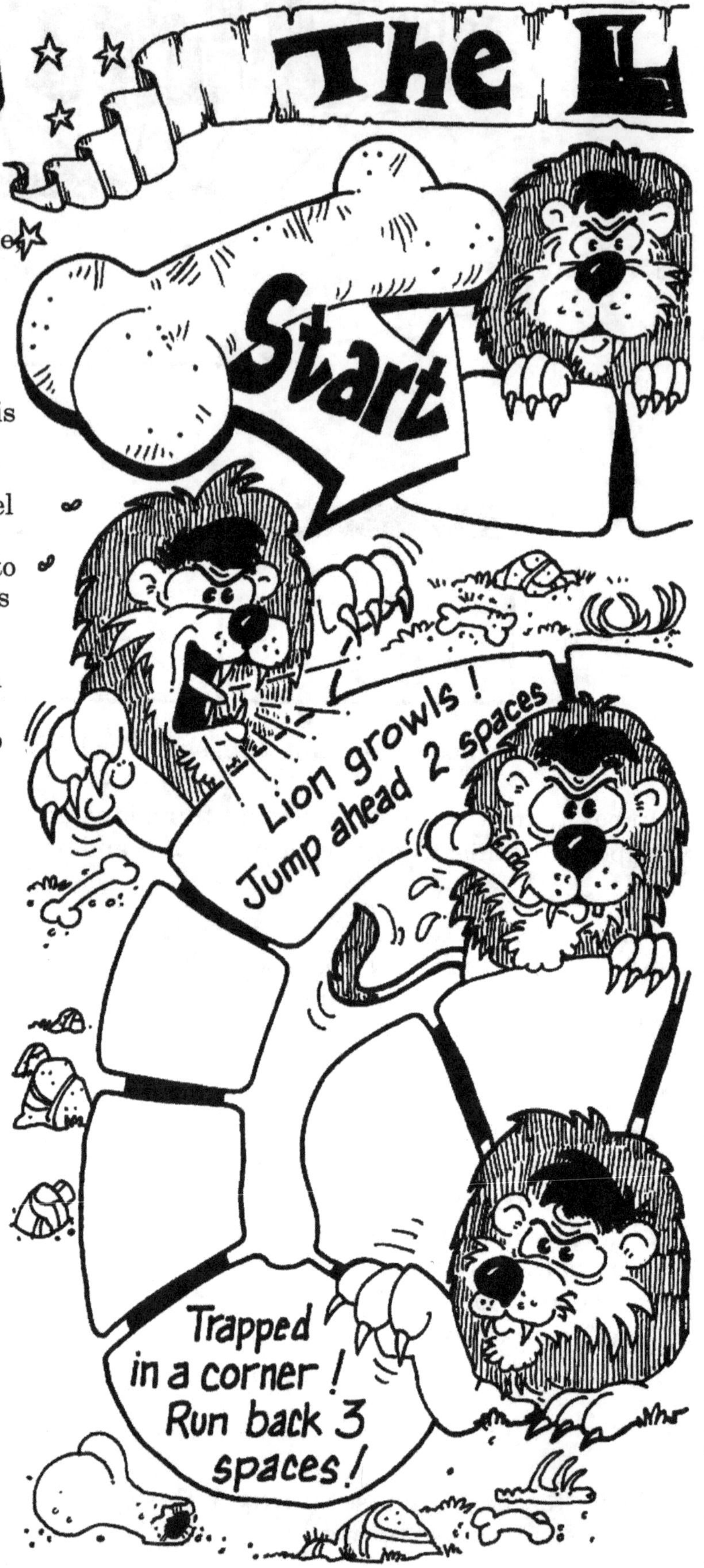
The L
Start
Lion growls ! Jump ahead 2 spaces
Trapped in a corner ! Run back 3 spaces !

**You Need:**
angel cards (below), game board, one die, place markers for each player

**Directions:**
1. Place markers at "Start" and give each player three angel cards.
2. Rolling the die, each player makes his or her way around the lions' den toward the exit door. A player who lands on a lion must turn in one angel card to save himself. If a player runs out of angels, he or she must return to "Start" and pick up three more angels to begin again.

Teacher/parent: Color (or have children color) the game board. Then mount the game on a file folder, and laminate it to use over and over !

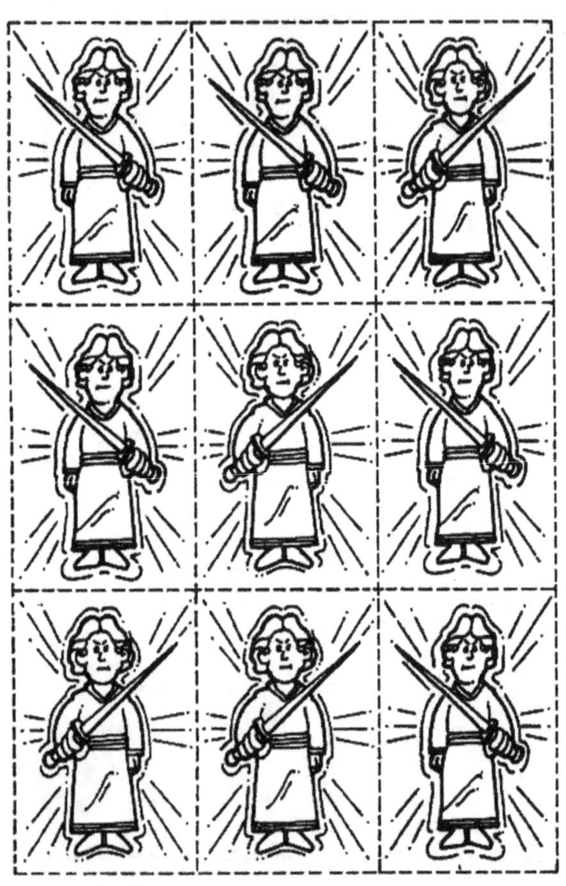

ions' Den
Whew! Whew! Sittin' 'tween two!
EXIT
Safe at Last

# Lions, Lions Everywhere!

Think of the most ferocious animal there is. Did you imagine a tiger or dinosaur? Chances are you also thought of a lion! When we think of places to see lions, we usually think of the jungles and plains of Africa. But did you know lions once roamed freely around the biblical lands where Abraham, Moses, David, Daniel, and even Jesus lived? Many years ago, various breeds of lions hunted in the hot, humid biblical lands of Palestine and the surrounding lands. Near East shepherds including Abraham and David were on constant look out for bears and lions that would attack the flocks of sheep and goats they tended. Armed with only spears and slings, shepherds would protect their flocks from wild lions using stones.

In the Bible, lions are often referred to as descriptions for power and strength, for evil, for crouching and hiding—and even for royalty as when Jesus is described as the *lion of Judah*—God's triumph and victory! Use the code below to fill in the missing words to Psalm 91:13 to see how victorious we are through God's power over evil.

| A | B | C | D | E | G | H |
|---|---|---|---|---|---|---|
| ● | ◊ | ✂ | ✦ | ◉ | ♦ | ✶ |
| | | | | | | |
| I | L | M | N | O | P | R |
| ✹ | ✕ | ⅄ | ✓ | ★ | ⊠ | ⊙ |
| | | | | | | |
| S | T | U | W | Y | | |
| + | ⟐ | ☾ | ⊗ | ▣ | | |

"

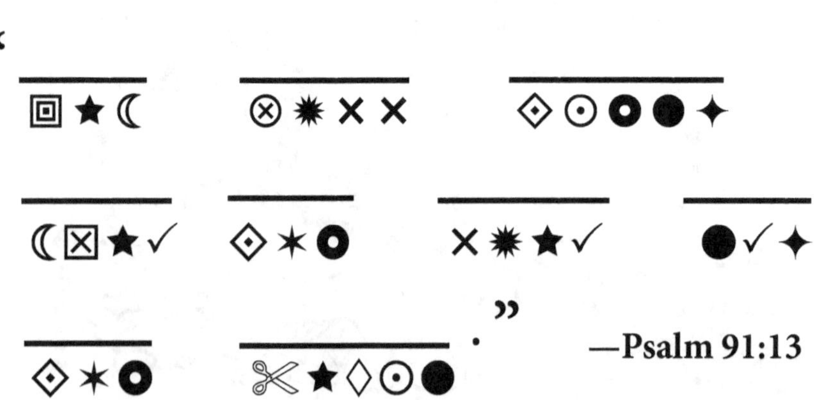

."

—Psalm 91:13

# Prayerful Daniel

Use your NIV Bible to look up **Romans 12:12** and fill in the missing words to this awesome memory verse to discover the good qualities Daniel filled his heart with. Then color the picture as you think about the good qualities God desires you to have in your life.

"Be

__________

in hope,

__________

in affliction,

__________

in prayer."

—Romans 12:12

**Open any window; open any door.
God has given us glorious gifts
to seek, to find, to explore!**

God's gift to Daniel was fiery faith which
Daniel returned through his prayers.
Draw a picture of a gift God has given you.

# Notes

www.ingramcontent.com/pod-product-compliance
Lightning Source LLC
LaVergne TN
LVHW080322110826
845155LV00026B/180

* 9 7 8 1 9 3 5 1 4 7 1 0 7 *